Services for Young Children with Working Mothers

REPORT
BY THE CENTRAL POLICY REVIEW STAFF

LONDON
HER MAJESTY'S STATIONERY OFFICE

ISBN 0 11 630805 2

SERVICES FOR YOUNG CHILDREN WITH WORKING MOTHERS

Report by the Central Policy Review Staff

TABLE OF CONTENTS

Services for Young Children with Working Mothers

INTRODUCTION

1. In 1975 the government published a CPRS study " A Joint Framework for Social Policy ". The report emphasised the need for better co-ordination in the development of social policy between government departments and between central government and local authorities. As part of the follow up Ministers asked the CPRS to carry out a number of studies of particular areas in the social policy field where it seemed likely that there were problems of co-ordination and where a more ' joint ' approach might be valuable. The CPRS reports on Population and the Social Services, and on the Relations between Central Government and Local Authorities have been published, and work is proceeding on housing and the social services. At the same time efforts have been made on the co-ordination of statistics within government to encourage the provision of the necessary information base for a more comprehensive approach to the development of social policy.

2. As a part of all this the CPRS was asked to look at the services provided for the children of working mothers. There had been a steady upward trend in the numbers of women at work who had young children and the CPRS was asked to consider what the implications of this were for social policy both for families, and for the young children in them.

3. The CPRS undertook the study at a time when the issue of the day care services for young children was under widespread discussion. It is a field in which there has been a considerable amount of research both in this country and abroad and on which there are very differing conclusions. For some time there have been signs of mounting political interest in these issues: both the role of women in employment and in their families, and the kind of intervention which the government should make in the care of young children. In the course of 1977 organisations working in the field produced several policy documents urging on the government a change in their approach to the services provided for children under school age.

A 2

4. In the course of the CPRS study we have made a series of visits to examine the provision which is made at present by both public, private and voluntary organisations for the care of children during the day. We have had discussions with those working in the field and have received written evidence both on existing conditions and on policy prescriptions for future developments. We have also been helped by both the central government departments involved with young children (primarily the Department of Health and Social Security and the Department of Education and Science) and also by the local authorities who are involved in providing services directly to those who use them. A list of the local authorities visited is in Annex 1.

5. In this report we discuss the role of the government in relation to families with young children and what form policies in this area might take. We have refrained from entering into the debate about whether or not mothers with young children should work but took as a fact that at the present time there are a large number of mothers with young children who do work. We have not undertaken any special research project as part of our study, apart from the statistical exercise necessary to estimate numbers of mothers with young children who work; we have however drawn on the research of others, of which there is a great deal in this field, particularly on children under five. Most of the statistical material is in the annexes.

Children aged 0—10 with mothers in paid employment, 1971 and 1976

Great Britain

1971 Total: 9.7m children

1976 Total: 8.8m children

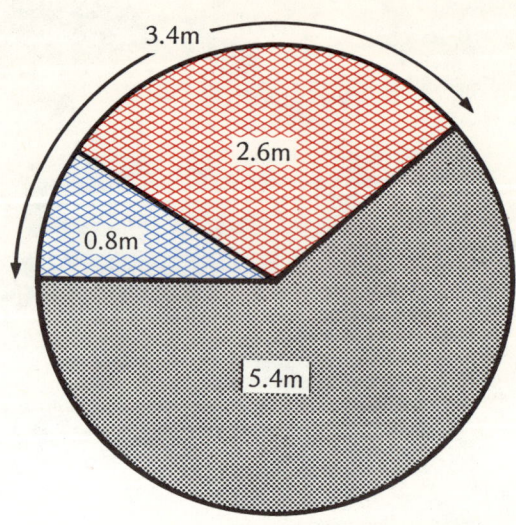

2.6m

1.8m

0.8m

7.1m

3.4m

2.6m

0.8m

5.4m

Children aged 0—4 with mothers in paid employment, 1971 and 1976

Great Britain

1971 Total: 4.4m children

1976 Total: 3.6m children

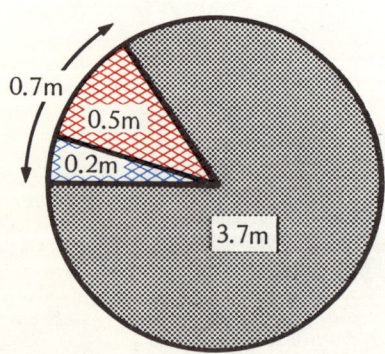

0.7m

0.5m

0.2m

3.7m

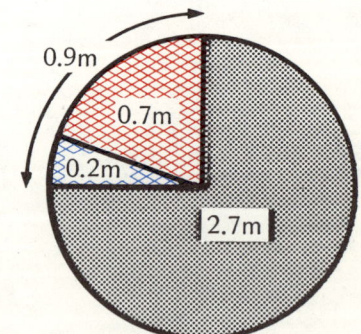

0.9m

0.7m

0.2m

2.7m

Children with mothers in full-time employment (over 30 hrs per week)

Children with mothers in part-time employment (30 hrs or less per week)

Children with mothers not in employment

Services for Young Children with Working Mothers

PART I: THE NEEDS OF FAMILIES

1.1 Most parents with young children need advice and help in caring for them and bringing them up. This advice and help is still provided mainly by immediate family and close friends but government agencies have an increasing role to play in providing the essential health and advisory services to help young parents. Parents who work face the additional difficulty of finding regular and competent care for their children. Although the Government has accepted the case for expanding part-time nursery education to meet children's needs, at present it does little to meet this need of working parents—most care for young children is still provided within extended families or in the private sector.

Working mothers

1.2 In spite of the lack of organised day care there has been, over recent decades, a major increase in the numbers of mothers with young children who work. Even in the five years between 1971 and 1976, when employment generally was falling the numbers of mothers with young children who had a job increased. For the purposes of this present study the Office of Population Censuses and Surveys and the Central Statistical Office undertook a special analysis of children with working mothers. Diagrams A and B show the proportions of children in Great Britain under 11 and under 5 with mothers in employment in 1971 and 1976. They show that in 1976 two fifths of all children under 11 and a quarter of children under five had mothers in paid employment compared with a quarter and a sixth only five years before.

1.3 A large proportion of these children have mothers who do part-time rather than full-time jobs—and it is in this area that the greater part of the increase in numbers has come. Nevertheless in 1976 it is estimated that there were about 200,000 children under 5 and 600,000 children between 5 and 10 whose mothers worked for over 30 hours a week.

Children under 5

1.4 There are at present some 900,000 children under 5 whose mothers work and who must either (i) make private arrangements for the care of their children with families or friends, or (ii) use childminders or private day nurseries, or (iii) fit their jobs around such provision as is made by the education service for children over three. Local authority social services departments provide full time day care for only 30,500 children under 5 in Great Britain, but these places have to meet all forms of need for day care, including family breakdown and children at risk of illtreatment, so that the places available for children with working parents, who have no other reason for priority treatment are few and far between. The demand for day nursery places is therefore far greater than the supply. At any one time there may be 12,000 children in England on waiting lists, many of whom will never get a place, but many other children are not put down on waiting lists because their chances of getting a place are so slight.

1.5 At present nursery education does not really provide for working mothers. In January 1977 in England there were nearly 200,000 children between 3 and 5 in nursery schools and classes, but normally for sessions of only 2–3 hours a day. There were also about 245,000 children under five in ordinary primary school classes of whom just over 140,000 were rising fives. The hours of the sessions are short and the holidays long. So alternative arrangements are invariably necessary to fill the gaps if the parent is to maintain a regular job.

1.6 Most working parents therefore use the services of a child-minder. Local authority social services departments register childminders and normally try to ensure that the service they provide is a reasonable one. In 1976 there were 63,000 full time and 20,000 part time registered places with childminders in England. The numbers of unregistered childminders are difficult to measure but estimates have ranged between 100,000 and 300,000.

1.7 From the figures sketched above it is clear that many working mothers must be using a mixture of methods of providing care for their children. The schools are little help and the day nurseries and childminders are not meeting the bulk of the needs of the 900,000 children under 5 whose mothers work. Nursery schools and playgroups as organised at present cannot provide the regularity of care which is essential for maintaining employment either full or part time. The traditional pattern has been for grandparents or other members of the family to carry out a considerable amount of caring for young children. But, as the proportions of older women returning to full time employment continue to increase, this source of assistance is becoming less readily available.

Children between 5 and 10

1.8 Parents with children of statutory school age but who are too young to look after themselves (between the ages of 5 and about 11) face a particularly difficult problem. During the school term it is perfectly possible for both parents to work during school hours but full time or permanent employment is difficult unless the parents are able to make alternative arrangements for the care of their children after school has finished and during the school holidays.

1.9 Such arrangements, are, if anything, harder to make than those for children under 5. Care is needed for perhaps two to three hours in the late afternoon for about 37 weeks in the year, and for a further ten to twelve weeks during the school holidays the care has to be full time. Again, in a large number of cases relations and friends give help; children spend the early evenings in other homes, with childminders or with their older siblings, and, not infrequently, on their own at home or out of doors waiting for their parents to return.

1.10 The holidays present even greater problems. There are, in some areas play centres and special activities, often provided by local authorities, but they seldom aim to occupy the children for a full working day. Holiday play schemes appear to be designed more as an antidote to boredom than as care for the children, even though they frequently are used by the children as " care " rather than as part-time activities. Furthermore, holiday play schemes cater mainly for secondary school children; those which cater for the needs of very young children (of " infant " and " junior " ages) are few and far between.

1.11 These difficulties faced by mothers with children of primary school age, who wish to work full time may well be the reason for the high proportion who work part time—the proportion of working mothers with school age children working full time is only slightly higher than for mothers with children under five.

Services for families

1.12 Parents who work also need access to a range of health and advisory services. Most of these services are still run on the assumption that mothers do not work—even though nearly half of them do. Health visitors and clinics normally operate only during

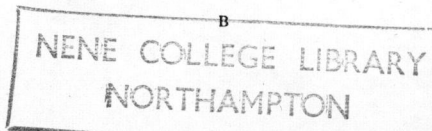

the day, and voluntary play groups and nursery schools operate only part time and for sessions which are geared to the needs of the children and the administration and not to those of working parents.

1.13 Parents, whether working or not, do need readily accessible sources of advice on the difficulties which can arise when bringing up small children. At present the advisory services are fairly formalised. Health visitors visit a young baby and its parents and will continue to visit if there is a clear need for support and the caseload is not too high. GP's and clinic medical officers give advice in ordinary surgeries and clinics. Social workers will help families suffering from identifiable crisis. In some areas young mothers can also go to " mother and baby " groups which provide support for young mothers as well as activities for the children.

1.14 The advisory functions provided by health visitors and GP's and social workers are obviously important for young parents dealing with small children for the first time. But the health profession is by no means the only source of advice and support. In many cases crucial initial advice is given by other professionals—teachers, day nursery matrons, or play group leaders as an informal, and frequently unrecognised, part of their work. The experience of the few " phone-in " experiments there have been, have indicated how desperate, in some cases, the need for accessible informal help sometimes is, and how significant it can be as preventative work.

1.15 The needs of parents, as individuals, get very little recognition from the formal structure of social services. The slow realisation of the problems of depressed and isolated mothers[1] is a clear indication of how much remains to be done in the field of supportive services. One of the more important benefits of the spread of playgroups and nursery classes is the opportunity they give to hard pressed parents to have a break from the demands of small children. By the age of three most children benefit from wider experience and companionship of their own age group, while their parents can, in many cases for the first time for some years, get some relief from the physical and emotional pressures of young children.

1.16 Some young children and their parents need specialised help and assistance as the recent report of the Warnock committee[2] has emphasised. If the children suffer from physical or mental handicap

---

[1] Professor G. Brown et al. Sociology Vol. 9, May 1975, pg. 225: Psychiatric disturbance among women.

[2] Special Educational Needs: The Report of the Committee of Enquiry into the Education of Handicapped Children and Young People, Command 7212. HMSO 1978.

or deprivation the needs of their parents for co-ordinated and coherent advice and support are very great. Most parents in these circumstances are heavily dependent on outside help to bring up their children in as satisfactory a way as possible. These services should be provided in a coherent and constructive way if the needs of those families are to be met.

1.17 Children coming from deprived or broken homes frequently need compensating assistance. But help which is aimed, for example, at assisting a 4 year old living in deplorable housing conditions needs to be matched by help for the parents in coping with the difficulties under which they have to labour, if the work with the child is not to be negated. Some children may also need special help because they have particular difficulties in speaking or in learning English or in coping with different cultural patterns.

Preventative work

1.18 Preventative work undertaken with under fives and their families can reduce the waste of expensive resources at a later stage, when the need to cope with the consequences of family stress and breakdown becomes more apparent and urgent, as the children are involved in delinquency, crime, truancy or exhibit emotional problems. Both the Court Report[1] on child health services and the Warnock Report on the handicapped have stressed the need for early preventative action to deal with both physical and mental deprivation in its widest sense.

---

[1] Fit for the Future; The Report of the Committee on Child Health Services, Command 6684. HMSO 1977.

PART II: GOVERNMENT POLICY

Priorities

2.1 In the United Kingdom, in 1976 about £850 million of public money was spent on health, education and social services for children under five in the United Kingdom (a detailed list is in Annex 7) but there is little indication of any underlying principle governing the way in which that expenditure was distributed. There are two major reasons for this. First, there is no clearly stated policy or programme on expenditure for this age group as a whole. The only recent substantial policy document, the 1972 Education White Paper 'A Framework for Expansion' has been overtaken by the subsequent public expenditure cuts. And this document was not a blue print for a programme of services for young children but suggested an increase in nursery education on traditional lines—mainly on a part-time basis. Second, the number of different programmes which are involved in services for the under-fives means that there are always conflicting priorities operating. One Government department may try to give high priority to its services for the under-fives; another will effectively give it no priority at all. At a local level these imbalances show up startlingly.

2.2 For children between 5 and 11 it is impossible to produce an expenditure figure corresponding to the £850 million for the under fives. The overlap between education and social services is far less apparent than for the younger age group so disparities in priority are less obvious.

Comment

2.3 The government needs to take a fundamental look at what services are now provided for young children, and what they should be. Hitherto the (convenient) assumption has been that the parents, and in particular the mother, can normally cope unaided with a child's first 5 years of life with a certain amount of fairly elementary help on health and development, together with some part time nursery education for children over three. Even this very limited provision is very far from universal. Nursery education is still only available for a minority and even cases of desperate need for day care are not all met.

2.4 However the assumption that in normal circumstances the family can cope is now no longer a sufficient answer. The social structure which at one time supported young parents—settled communities and an extended family—is no longer available to increasing numbers of young working parents.

Inequality

2.5 The needs of young children are not the complete responsibility of any one central government department and the facts of bureaucratic life are such, that this means that they almost inevitably take second place behind those policies for which any department has sole charge, or for which it has mandatory responsibility.

2.6 Local priorities tend to be determined by the enthusiasm of individual officers and elected members. Individual problems of young children and their families, unlike for example the disabled or the elderly, alter quickly with time and soon become the responsibility of another department. The under-five with a social problem rapidly becomes the adolescent with a social problem and solutions have to be found elsewhere. Unless rapid results can be expected, therefore, those who bring pressure on local authorities to act in this area, do so from altruistic motives alone or give up the battle when their own children can no longer benefit. In particular those parents who need full-time day care are frequently inarticulate with neither the time nor the energy for pressure group activity. Arguments about the importance of local democracy in social policy have therefore less force in this area.

2.7 Annex 5 sets out the number and proportions of places for under fives for all local authorities. In one area a child may benefit from a well co-ordinated, well organised and reasonably funded service. In another area only the work of voluntary associations can provide a reasonable spread of pre-school activities for children of 3 and above, and in yet another area there may be virtually no help or assistance whatever to parents and their families no matter how great their needs may be. The figures in Annex 5 show, for example, that the London Borough of Waltham Forest provides 18·9 day nursery places for every 1000 children under five, and Islington 61·6. The disparities are as great in nursery education: Essex provides 4·5 full time and 11·6 part time places in nursery schools and classes per 1000, while Hertfordshire (with a similar rate of provision of playgroup places) has 8·6 full time and 93·1 part time places per 1000 under fives.

Demands for a change in policy by pressure groups

2.8 The present system has produced many demands for a change in policy. In the course of 1977 and 1978 policy documents dealing with policies for the under-fives have been produced by, among others, the Association of Metropolitan Authorities and the Association of County Councils, the TUC, the National Campaign for Nursery Education, the Pre-School Playgroups Association and the National Union of Teachers. Local organisations have also mounted powerful and in many cases effective lobbies against proposals to cut back services to the under-fives as part of the cuts in public expenditure. The case that is made varies in emphasis but almost all of them argue that there would be substantial benefits to both children and parents in a major expansion of provision for young children.

2.9 There is also extensive research evidence on the demands of parents with young children. For example, the Office of Population Censuses and Surveys published recently[1] a survey of the needs of mothers with children under five which showed substantial unsatisfied demand for improved services, particularly for day care. It was clear that the parents themselves felt that the services provided for them were inadequate and in many cases seriously so. Studies of particular projects have also shown a remarkable response by parents to experimental schemes which provided more extensive help. For example the National Education Research and Development Trust experiments with the Child Care Switchboard—a 24 hour phone-in service for parents—produced a substantial response, which indicated the extent to which parents needed, in some cases desperately, a simple, informal and accessible form of support and reassurance.

Prevention

2.10 The general recognition of the importance of the experiences of children during their first five years, lends force to the argument that the sooner preventative help can be given to both parents and children, the higher the chances are that crises can either be avoided, or those involved can be helped more effectively to cope with crisis when it occurs. Large sums of public money are already spent in dealing with the consequences of damage to children in their early years. The simple financial cost of non-accidental injury to children, family breakup and the depressive illnesses connected with isolated child rearing are all very considerable, quite apart from the incalculable cost of misery and suffering. The longer term cost of dealing

[1] Pre-school children and their need for day care. Margaret Bone: OPCS 1977.

with the emotional problems of older children and with learning difficulties and education failure are all important factors which can be mitigated by more preventative work at an earlier stage.

The government's role

2.11 The issue is not, as is frequently supposed, whether the government should be involved at all in so domestic a relationship as that between parents and a pre-school child, where there are no obvious social inadequacies. The real question is whether the government's existing role is sufficient, given the intrinsic importance of ensuring that young children in our society have adequate attention paid to their needs.

2.12 At present the administrative responsibility for services to the under-fives is divided between a number of different agencies. (Annex 4 discusses the details and the administration of the services.) There is virtually no overall co-ordination of policies or practices and this lack of co-ordination is exceedingly obvious in the service provided to the families concerned. It is inevitable in this kind of situation that resources are wasted. Local authorities have parallel organisations dealing with similar problems and frequently dealing with the same customers. The administrative divisions are exacerbated by the professional divisions, and, while the professional divisions, in some cases, represent genuinely different approaches to different needs, in many cases they form a barrier to useful communication and co-operation on common problems.

2.13 The divisions within local authorities are further compounded by the divisions between central government departments. At present the co-ordination by central government departments is mainly limited to exchanging information. Exhortations to local authorities to plan such services as they have in a co-ordinated manner lack conviction when the co-ordinated approach to central planning consists mainly in duplicating documents. The circular issued recently (Annex 6) exemplifies the present confusion. It encourages local authorities to plan jointly but without giving any indication of a parallel move by the central government departments concerned where major issues of policy and financing are involved.

What is wrong

2.14 There are four main aspects of the services for children where existing policies are inadequate:

    (*a*) There is a lack of direction and no clear priorities as to the ways in which services should progress.

(*b*) There is confusion in the administration of services for children under five. The provision of services is fragmented and responsibility is divided.

(*c*) The consequences of the present situation for the children and their parents are both unjust and inequitable. There is a serious lost opportunity for preventative work at an early stage.

(*d*) It is widely recognised that children benefit from some education and care outside their homes between the ages of three and five. A substantial number of children are denied this benefit because adequate provision is not available.

PART III : RECOMMENDATIONS

3.1   In any proposals for changes in the present system of providing services for families with young children, three main principles need to be followed.

3.2   First, flexibility: inevitably needs will vary from one area of the country to another and from one period in time to another depending on the age structure of the community, the employment patterns in the areas, and the resources which the community itself can provide.   Any reorganisation must remain sufficiently flexible to take account of these variations.

3.3   Second, no reorganisation unless it is essential: the present system may have many unsatisfactory features but even within the existing pattern there are areas of the country where a reasonable degree of co-ordination of the services is already being achieved. In recent years local authorities have undergone considerable up-heaval: any further reorganisation should be undertaken only as a last resort.   The policy should be to build, wherever possible, on what we already have.   But where the present system is not adequate some reorganisation will be required.

3.4   Third, the crucial role of the professional worker: to a very large extent it is the professional workers who have the expertise which is necessary to help families with young children.   It is the professionals who provide the support, advice and encouragement which should be the primary service available.   Much of their work in this area should be advisory and supportive.   There are times when professionals need to give clear guidance and provide services. But wherever possible their role should be one of supporting and encouraging parents to be independent, to take decisions themselves and make arrangements themselves rather than lean increasingly on services provided for them by someone else.   The objective of encouraging self-help wherever possible has been adopted in some local authority areas; but for many professional workers it is an approach which involves some basic rethinking.   This is particularly true of those who are now training professional groups for the future.

Services for young families

3.5   We have identified four main areas where families with young children need services:

(*a*) day care for children under 5

(b) nursery education for children under 5

(c) after-school and holiday care for children between 5 and 10

(d) advisory and supportive services.

3.6 It could be said that in an ideal world all of these would be provided by a single cohesive service for families with young children. But to do this would require major local and central government reorganisation. The policy of " building on what we have " implies retention of different services but the development of a much higher degree of co-ordination between them.

I. Day care for children under 5

3.7 At present there are major problems of child neglect and the widespread use of unsatisfactory childminders. The aim is the establishment of a suitable day care service readily available to parents who need it. The most satisfactory position would be a statutory obligation on all local authorities to ensure adequate day care in their area. Progress towards this goal would need to depend on local circumstances including, of course, the availability of resources.

3.8 The pattern of day care which is most appropriate in a local area will vary from place to place but the task of each local authority would be to see that, taken together, the facilities provided by the private sector, the voluntary sector and the local authority itself were adequate for local needs.

3.9 At present the main effort of most local authorities on day care is in the provision of day nurseries for children in special need. This has always been the first priority and must remain so. That is to say, the first call on any extra resources must be to improve the coverage for the existing priority categories. There is a strong case for providing these resources as a matter of urgency. But the contribution which the local authority itself makes to day care provision in its area should not be limited to the expansion of the traditional day nursery. In day nurseries the need to provide catering facilities and a full time trained staff with a higher ratio of staff to children means both high capital costs and high running costs. These expensive day nurseries will continue to be necessary for children who need specialist attention and provision for these special cases is still far from adequate. But for other children local authorities could, at far less expense, extend childminder services for the younger children and increase the provision of places in nursery classes for older children.

3.10 It is estimated that there are nearly 900,000 children under 5 in Great Britain whose mothers work full or part time. Local authority day nurseries and registered child minders provide only about 120,000 full and part time places; although not all working mothers need day care there is still a long way to go in providing an adequate service. One obvious way in which part of the gap could be filled is to use more intensively the facilities of the nursery schools. Nursery classes are normally open for two sessions between 9 a.m. and 3.30 p.m. Many mothers work part time for between 20 and 30 hours a week. They need help looking after their children for times which do not fit into the normal nursery school hours and they need help also during the school holidays. Recent experiments have shown that at comparatively little cost the nursery school sessions can be extended for another two or three hours until parents are able to come and collect their children when their working day is finished.

3.11 Perhaps the most common form of day care is child minding. Bad child minding can have social consequences which are both difficult and expensive to try to set right, and the present service is inadequate and piecemeal. The needs are to get the maximum number of child minders registered with local authorities and for local authorities then to give the child minders help and support. At present the status of child minders is low yet the contribution they can make to adequate child care is large. A trained child minder should be regarded by professional workers in the field as a colleague with valuable experience and knowledge. The remuneration of child minders should increasingly reflect this and, as resources permit, local authorities could develop schemes for child minding while recouping a substantial part of the cost from those parents who are able to pay for it.

II. Pre-school education for children 3 to 5

3.12 The advantages of nursery education for children from 3 to 5 are widely recognised and accepted by the Government. The ultimate objective should be to make it readily available to all who want it, and to encourage parents to send their children so that they will benefit educationally. As with day care, the most satisfactory step might be a statutory obligation on local authorities to provide part-time pre-school education on demand, from 3 to 5, though the introduction of this would obviously have to be phased over time. Again, as with day care, demand will vary from area to area and local authorities, in consultation with local parents, would need to decide how extensive provision should be including the ratio of full-time to part-time places. But it is desirable that ultimately virtually all children should have had some school experience before the age of five, if only part time.

3.13 Nursery education absorbs a substantial proportion of expenditure on under fives. But the form in which it is provided—short sessions and long holidays—means that it is of little use to many of the mothers and children who need it most. More extended hours and longer sessions in nursery schools would mean that more children who need it could benefit and would not have to make the adjustment of going straight from home to infant school at the age of five. In a flexible system children in day nurseries, or with child minders should be encouraged to make use of the facilities of nursery schools. Also, in a co-ordinated system, there should be teachers on the staff of the day nurseries, as the norm rather than the exception, and strong links between the primary schools and the day nurseries should help to bridge the transition of the older children to the primary schools.

3.14 A flexible and more co-ordinated service should help the nursery education sector reorientate itself towards the needs of working parents. At the moment we have an expensive and somewhat inflexible system of nursery education which is still, in too many cases, of little help to the working mother. She has to do the best she can elsewhere and the alternatives she can find are often far from satisfactory. A cheaper and more flexible system aimed more at the needs of the working mother is an important reorientation of priorities.

3.15 The term 'pre-school education' for the under fives needs to be interpreted in the widest sense. For example, the play group movement is extremely valuable in giving children (particularly the younger children) and their parents, experience outside the home. The extension of nursery school education should not lead to the abandonment of play groups. Nursery classes and play groups should work together and, in particular, should help strengthen a closer and more constructive relationship between teachers and young parents. As nursery education expands the role of the play groups could be developed to concentrate especially on the younger ages, including those under three, whose needs are at present less recognised than those between 3 and 5. Until expansion is fully under way play groups are one way of utilising spare accommodation in primary schools resulting from the fall in the birth rate. And local authorities could find this a valuable means of encouraging their voluntary sector. There is an interesting example at Crewe where a local play group effectively acts as a nursery class for a local primary school, using empty classrooms on the school premises and having close informal links with the primary school itself. It provides continuity for the children between their nursery activities and their primary school, and makes it possible for them to have some pre-school experience before the age of five in a district which has little nursery education on classic lines.

III. After school and holiday care for children 5 to 10

3.16 The school day and the school year seldom coincide with the working day and the working year of the mother. Children leave school earlier in the afternoon and their holidays are longer. While these differences persist the problems will remain. A survey carried out some two years ago by the Association of Municipal Authorities, the Association of County Councils, and the Convention of Scottish Local Authorities showed that the efforts made to fill this gap are seldom adequate for working parents. The schemes were largely organised by the local education authorities (occasionally jointly with the social service departments—the social service departments in a few cases ran schemes on their own). The typical scheme provides activities for three to four weeks in the school summer holidays. The main purpose was to help the children educationally or socially by providing for example constructive entertainment for children in deprived areas; they were not aimed primarily to help working mothers.

3.17 These schemes could be substantially expanded especially in socially deprived areas, such as the inner cities, and in areas with a high proportion of women in employment. The school is the obvious and sensible place to locate the schemes, avoiding the problem of unfamiliar surroundings and further travel for the younger children after school. Existing buildings would be used and, for after-school facilities, staff of suitable background and experience should be recruited and paid on an hourly basis. They need not be qualified teachers, for the purpose of these sessions is not to add extra education but to leave children in the care of a responsible adult. Suitable opportunities for rest and recreation such as the children would have at home should be available, for example books, television and a snack. In a school holiday scheme however some qualified staff (either teachers, youth, or community workers) are required. But support staff can as at present be students or, in some cases, parents. The statutory powers[1] under which

[1] Education Act 1944 (Section 53); Children and Young Persons Act 1963 (Section 1).

provision is made at present for children of school age are not entirely satisfactory and legislation is required to clarify these powers and to extend them.

3.18 To provide cost effective management and continuity the administrative structure for the establishment and running of these after school and holiday schemes for the 5–10's should be similar to that proposed for services for children under five.

3.19 At present the biggest problem is shortage of money and while demand exceeds supply priority should be given to the following groups:

(i) Single parents in employment

(ii) Parents where one or other is physically or mentally ill or handicapped

(iii) Families with grossly inadequate housing

(iv) Families with other social problems referred by social workers

(v) Families where both parents are in full-time or nearly full-time employment

(vi) Single parents who are not seeking employment.

The scale of after-school provision should not normally be greater than is necessary to provide for these priority groups. However, especially in socially deprived areas such as the inner cities, school holiday provision should where possible be extended to the non-priority groups for at least part of the holidays. Resources under the Inner City Partnership Schemes might be used for this purpose.

3.20 Local authorities are on the whole reluctant to impose charges for provision of this kind. But as with child minding there is no reason in principle why means-tested charges should not be made particularly if a substantial number of children with two parents at work are being catered for. In some low income areas the administrative costs of collecting what are, after means-testing, small amounts may not justify charging. Policies on charging should therefore be left to the discretion of individual authorities.

3.21 The extension of this after school and holiday provision would provide at relatively little cost much needed support for working parents, especially those who are single. It would in addition help:

(i) the reduction of road accidents and other types of accident to children alone at home or on the streets

(ii) the reduction of vandalism resulting from school holiday boredom (more and more vandalism is committed by young children)

(iii) reductions in other types of delinquency

(iv) opportunities for children to develop skills and participate in educationally stimulating activities in the school holidays.

IV. Advisory and Supportive Services

3.22 Local authorities and health authorities need to work together to provide adequate advisory services for parents of young children so that parents who need help and support are able to get it. At an early stage in the child's life advice should be provided by clinics and health visitor services to introduce parents to the professional services which are available to them.

3.23 Local authorities and health authorities should be encouraged to provide a range of services for parents as resources permit. For example, a telephone advisory service, provided as part of the health visitor and social work service and available outside normal working hours, gives parents somewhere to turn in a crisis. It would obviously be unnecessary to provide help for all families with children but the service should have as its aim the meeting of real need for advice and should develop a sufficiently flexible system to be able to respond both to the urgent needs of families under stress and to the day to day concerns of young parents coping particularly with a first child. Priority for the provision of any service would be given to families coping with real crisis; nevertheless if the important preventative benefits of this kind of advisory service are to be gained it should have sufficient resources to provide advice and support for families who, though worried, are not undergoing an immediate crisis.

3.24 Isolation and depression among mothers with small children and particularly in single parent families is surprisingly widespread. More could be done to encourage local groups of parents and young children, preferably organised by the parents themselves. These provide both support and companionship for the parents as much as an outlet for the activities of the children. The work of the voluntary associations could be particularly valuable here.

3.25 Local authorities could make more imaginative use of their existing facilities, for example, day nurseries could provide an advisory service for parents in their neighbourhood. More nursery schools could encourage both parents and young children to use their facilities. More local community associations and churches could, as part of their work, make provision for isolated parents with very young children.

3.26 In some areas this kind of activity is already taking place. Its extension need not involve high capital expenditure nor, after an initial period, need it occupy a great deal of expensive professional time. The capacities of communities to provide their own facilities obviously vary from place to place but the resources which organisations like the PPA have tapped within the community should be an encouragement to local authorities to work more by providing advice and support for small local groups rather than take over the full administrative responsibility.

Organisation and Administration

3.27 Given their existing organisation both local authorities and central departments would in many instances find it difficult to provide a co-ordinated service on the lines suggested above. The provision of care and education is complicated both by the division of administrative responsibilities and by differences in approach on the part of the different professional groups involved. The weakness of the division of responsibility within Whitehall makes it difficult to co-ordinate services centrally. Alternative approaches to better co-ordination are discussed below. One would involve a simple functional split at the age of 3—the age at which most children become more independent of their parents and ready for communal activity—between the two major departments concerned (DHSS and DES). The second is to work with the existing system but to impose a higher degree of co-ordinated planning and expenditure both locally and within Whitehall.

Responsibility split by age

3.28 The first option would operate centrally by giving DHSS responsibility for children up to the age of 3 and then making 3 and 4 year olds the responsibility of DES. In local government social service departments would be responsible for under threes and local education authorities would extend their competence from 5–16 down to three and four year olds, both for nursery education and for extended day care in schools.

3.29 For the under 3's social services departments would have a responsibility together with the health authorities for providing advisory services to parents of very young children and providing support and day care where this was needed. At 3 the responsibility for children and their parents would pass to the education department (except in special cases where there was some reason for continued social services involvement).

3.30 There would be problems of overlap, for example in the provision of advisory services and regulatory services for childminders, and for day care for children from 3–5 where the local education authority was unable to meet the need for intensive support.

3.31 At the local level this structure would involve a fairly radical reshaping of both the education and social services provision for under-fives. Nevertheless it would ensure that more of the services for each age group were provided by a single institution and could be co-ordinated sensibly both at local and central level.

3.32 The advantages of the ‘ split ’ option seem to be outweighed by its disadvantages. The division of responsibility at the age of three would be a fairly artificial one (although in many ways no more so than at present) and the difficulties of overlap would be considerable. Furthermore, as we have argued, the expertise needed to run the services above and below 3 is similar, not distinct; a sharp break at a certain age would probably serve to encourage duplication of professional resources rather than their better use. A reorganisation of this kind would also be a major upheaval for the services concerned, which would probably be unpopular with both sides. Its main advantage, administrative simplicity, would be greatly outweighed by these factors.

Co-ordinated responsibility

3.33 The second option, and the one which we commend to Ministers, is to build on the work being done already to encourage and foster co-ordination between the two main service departments involved. One way of doing this is by setting up a joint policy group with collective joint responsibility for the new services.

3.34 At the local authority level there should be joint policy committees for children under 10, with equal representation from social service departments, from education departments, and advisers from the Area Health Authorities. These policy committees would cover the provision of advice, support, development and care, and the provision of pre and post statutory school age extended day services. They would need close links with those responsible for services for special groups—the handicapped and the deprived, and with the statutory education service.

3.35 The aim would be the achievement of common basic standards for the provision of services with a requirement that demand within the local area should be met within the reasonable constraints of time, money and flexibility.

3.36 In principle, finance should be found over time for establishing this scale and pattern of services through the ordinary Rate Support Grant machinery. But, in view of the widely differing provision in different local authority areas, the administrative complications, and the importance of the problem nationally, it may well be unwise to rely on the normal machinery. If Ministers were to take this view, they would need to consider a special block allocation of finance outside existing programme lines as a pump priming grant. Local Authorities would be required to produce a plan for their policies for young children before the special financing was agreed to.

3.37 Centrally there should be a joint unit (staffed by the Department of Education & Science and the Department of Health and Social Security) responsible for overseeing policies and expenditure for young children. The allocation of responsibility for this joint unit to the Ministers of State from both DES and DHSS would help to mark its importance. The policy of the unit would be to encourage local flexibility on the kind of response made but to ensure that basic standards were met and general guidelines followed.

3.38 There are already signs that a certain amount of co-ordination is being operated successfully within the present system. Some local authorities have produced joint planning documents on services for the under fives and others have set up joint planning teams of officials and elected members. Central government departments too are beginning to make moves in the direction of rather more co-ordinated planning. In some cases then the establishment of the system proposed here would pose few difficulties for local authorities. In others it might mean a considerable rethinking of departmental objectives and take some time to achieve.

Co-ordination with Health Authorities

3.39 The main responsibility for the development of services for children would fall on the social services and education departments of local authorities. But an important part has to be played by the health authorities. The role of professional health workers—doctors, health visitors and district nurses in work with young families is often insufficiently recognised. It is they who often see the first signs of difficulty and stress and devote time to advice and support.

The difficulties of co-ordination between the health authorities and local authority departments are well known and well documented, but co-ordination is essential if the real benefits of the service are to be obtained.

Costs

3.40 This report proposes an extensive development of the services for young children: the needs are obvious but the cost is a major factor. The services which are available at present are extremely expensive per capita both in initial capital costs and in running costs.

3.41 At present in Great Britain there are over three quarters of a million children under 5 whose mothers work and who have at present no access to local authority day nursery or child-minder provision. Not all these three quarters of a million would require full time day nursery care but the prohibitive cost of providing for even half a million places on the present basis is shown by the calculation that at 1975 prices the capital needed would be £1,750 million and the running costs £500 million. It is for this reason that we have suggested that the new service for young children should use the considerable non-professional resources within the community as much as possible rather than continue to provide a small and highly professional service for a few children. This implies a substantial change in present policies, requiring a change in emphasis from expensive services for a small number to a reasonable service for a much larger number. The new policy would certainly require additional public expenditure to operate it fully, but costs per head would be much lower than under the present system, as the estimates below demonstrate very strikingly.

3.42 On the capital side falling primary school numbers provide an opportunity for developing the provision of pre-school education and extended hours facilities for comparatively little. Encouragement of the voluntary sector and private childminder services should make it possible for local authorities to extend the quality and quantity of care for parents and their children comparatively cheaply.

Capital Costs

3.43 In 1975 the average capital cost of a place at a day nursery was £3,400. By 1978 this cost will have risen to nearer £4,000. By contrast the capital cost of a nursery school place in 1975–6 was only £910, and the capital cost of converting the existing premises (*e.g.* surplus primary school space) to accommodation suitable for nursery use was £310. These differences in capital costs between day nurseries and nursery classes are extraordinary. Day nurseries look after children for longer hours than nursery schools and need more accommodation, space and equipment. But this can hardly justify the expenditure of three times as much money in a field where resources are severely strained and desperate need goes unmet.

Running costs

3.44 In 1975 the running costs of a place at a day nursery were £1,000 a year. A place at a nursery school cost £750 and a place at a nursery class in an infants school cost £400—because of reduced administrative expenses. The costs of places with childminders and play groups were much lower—between £150 and £350 a year, mainly because rates of pay are so much lower.

3.45 Not only are day nurseries so very much more expensive but the blanket provision of day nursery facilities would not necessarily be the best solution to the needs of the children. A large proportion —about 80%—of mothers with young children work for 30 hours or less a week; flexible part time provision, rather than full time would meet most of their needs. For mothers with children between 3 and 5 nursery school provision would probably meet most needs, provided the hours were flexible and the school holidays were covered. There are about 400,000 such children whose mothers work part-time. To provide new nursery places for these children by converting primary school accommodation could cost (at 1975 prices) some £150m of capital and £250m of current cost. The demand however would be for less than an additional 400,000 places because of existing nursery places.

3.46 For the 400,000 under 3's with working mothers, properly trained and supported childminders are at their best and are by far the most economical form of support. A contribution to equipment and the provision of adequate training should go a long way to enabling childminders to provide such a service. For example an equipment grant and training cost of £200 for each childminder—even if she only looked after two children could provide facilities for 200,000 children for £20 million.

Special cases

3.47 There is one area where precise numbers are difficult to establish but the needs are urgent. These are the children in the priority categories who are or should be in local authority day nurseries now. The provision of day care for these children should be given very high priority. Day nursery places for the 12,000 children who were on the waiting lists in 1976 would cost £42 million at 1975 prices in capital costs and £12 million in current costs (considerably less if some of the need was met by adequately trained and supported childminders).

3.48 The costs given above are only illustrative of the kind of resources which could be involved in providing an adequate service of day care for children under five, using the existing pattern of services. We have also recommended that over time nursery education should be available to all children of 3 and 4 and that local authorities should develop adequate advisory and support services for families with young children. In some places the voluntary and private sector would be able to provide for a high proportion of demand at very little cost to public expenditure. In other areas where need is high and community resources low considerable resources would be necessary to provide an adequate service.

3.49 The cost of extended day provision (after hours care) for primary school children ought not to be great, if the objectives of the provision remain modest and untrained staff are used wherever possible for the two to three hours for which arrangements are necessary.

3.50 At present a great deal of experiment and improvisation goes into the patchwork of provision for young children, but the capacity of the system to develop without additional resources is small. Provision for young children has been cut, in some places heavily, in recent years; so any new major initiative will need resources to produce results. But in the short term these resources do not need to be large. The development of a comprehensive and co-ordinated service will take time, and patience, and can only be introduced as resources are available. With that proviso provision of an earmarked sum for capital and current expenditure rising to, say, £150 million a year over two to three years, initially for a period of five years (especially if it was used mainly for adapting existing buildings and to tap the capacities and expertise of parents and the voluntary sector) could well transform the provision of services for young children and make a substantial difference to the lives of a very large number of families. After the five year programme was completed the financing arrangements would have to be reviewed and, probably the current costs should then form part of the normal Rate Support Grant machinery.

Charging

3.51 Charging for services for children has always presented problems. At present parents are charged a fee for a place at a day nursery which is means tested but which, even when the maximum fee is charged, often bears little or no relation to the true cost of the place. Similarly parents whose child has a place with a salaried childminder are normally charged at the equivalent day nursery rate rather than the true cost of the place. Parents whose children go to nursery schools pay nothing, except the cost of school meals, and this charge is subject to the normal rules about the provision of free meals. Playgroups charge the parents a small fee but there are frequently arrangements for local authorities to sponsor places to meet the cost for poorer parents. Put baldly, the existing system means that parents getting full time day care in a day nursery—and that usually means parents in desperate social as well as financial need—pay for it, and parents who can get a place at a nursery class will get it free.

3.52 This situation needs to be rationalised. One way would be to abolish fees for day nurseries but to charge for meals (subject to the same qualification as for school meals). This would ensure equity between day nurseries and nursery schools while continuing to require at least a contribution for food from those parents who could afford it. However, if local authorities are required to make arrangements for day care for all parents who want it, there will be many who can well afford to make a substantial contribution to the cost. At present many already do so by employing childminders.

3.53 Perhaps the best course would be for local authorities to make a charge subject to a means test for child care related to the hours provided for all the places it provides, in day nurseries, with childminders or for the extended hours element in schools, both for nursery classes and after the end of the primary school day.

PART IV : CONCLUSIONS

4.1 The two main findings of this study are that :

(a) In Great Britain there are some 900,000 children under five whose mothers have a job; the government provides or controls full and part time day care for about 120,000 children in day nurseries and with child minders. There are a further two and a half million children between the ages of five and ten whose mothers work and for whom virtually no provision is made outside school hours.

(b) Such services as there are involve a wasteful use of resources by providing a service which is expensive per capita and yet is aimed at dealing with only a part of the needs of the children concerned.

The main recommendation of the study is that the two major services for young children: day nurseries and nursery education should be reorganised so that both institutions meet the needs of the children concerned for education *and* care rather than maintaining the existing divisions.

4.2 The objective is to provide young families with a reasonably co-ordinated service of care, education and support. It is also an objective to create some kind of order and equity out of the *ad hoc* services provided at the moment. A single co-ordinated service ought to make better use both of existing resources and of any additional resources which are made available. We have emphasised the importance of the preventative element in work with young children and their families, both in the provision of formal care and education services, and in the ready availability of help and advice. The developments we have suggested should go some way towards improving the conditions under which young children are brought up.

4.3 At present the government is spending very large sums of money indeed on support and assistance for older children for education and training (including further and higher education). In any society this kind of expenditure is both right and necessary. But services for younger children have been neglected and even curtailed. Young children do not, as yet, have any high political priority and their needs tend to be regarded as optional extras in the main programmes. The inadequacy of services for young children is bound to affect the kind of education and social provision which has to be made for them as they grow older, and the use they are able to make of the educational services available. Some of the extra money necessary to improve the services for young children and their parents could be found by reordering priorities within the education budget to ensure that young children receive greater recognition of their needs. For example, if half the additional £150 million, which this report proposes should be spent on services for young children, were to be found from existing education expenditure, it would involve a reordering of priorities within that programme of under 1 per cent. The fall in the child population makes it easier to do this now than at other times.

4.4 The service we have outlined could not, in any case, be implemented overnight. Its development will need careful thought and planning by both central and local government; but this means that preliminary planning should start as a matter of urgency. A certain amount can be done without much extra expenditure by improving existing administrative arrangements and making more imaginative use of existing resources. However, a reasonable and secure block of capital and current finance needs to be made available over a period of years to enable expansion to take place and planning to be undertaken in a realistic way. The type of ear-marked grant we have proposed has a prototype in the Urban Programme which has proved a reasonably flexible way of developing a particular programme for specific areas. There are already some experiments going on in the area of services for under fives and there are local authorities who would have little difficulty in submitting comprehensive plans for services for young children fairly rapidly.

4.5 The organisational changes we have proposed for central government are perhaps the most difficult to implement. We have suggested a unified policy group, outside existing departmental boundaries but with close links with the departments traditionally involved in this area and with Ministerial oversight from both main departments. We recognise that this is, at best, an organisational device for coping with the existing unsatisfactory demarcation. It is in no sense designed to be the precursor of a ' Minister for Children '. We do not consider that such a minister could play an effective role in the development of policy; at best he or she would have little more than a representational function. We envisage both the special grant and the unified policy group as a temporary measure to ensure that the service develops properly and smoothly from the start. The longer term future of both financing and policy would be best considered when the programme has been running for several years. It would then be essential to review the effectiveness of the programme and to consider how these services for young children should continue to be developed in the longer term.

4.6 One of the most important elements of the new service would be that local authorities should be urged to be flexible both in the resources that they use to meet needs in the community and in the kind of advice and help which is provided. There would however be a set of common standards which all local authorities would be expected to meet and which would ensure that parents and children throughout the country could rely on a reasonable level of service wherever they lived. Initially highest priority would need to be given to the many young children who for social reasons urgently need day care.

4.7 The arrangements proposed would make demands both on financial resources and on the people involved in providing the service. Although the cost of providing a full service on the lines we have recommended would be considerable, the CPRS consider that the needs of young families are such that the scale of expenditure we have proposed on a special programme over the next 7 to 8 years is justified both to remove the existing inequities, and in the longer term, to improve the conditions under which young children in this country are brought up.

ANNEX 1

We visited several local authorities for discussions about their policy on children under five, and children under 11 outside school hours, and saw a number of nurseries, nursery schools, day centres and play-groups in operation.   Our main visits were to:

Buckinghamshire

Cardiff

Cheshire

Edinburgh

Hampshire

ILEA

Lambeth

Leicester

Newham

Nottingham

Richmond

Sheffield

Southwark

Strathclyde

Westminster

Wiltshire

Children aged 0–10, 1956–1976
Great Britain

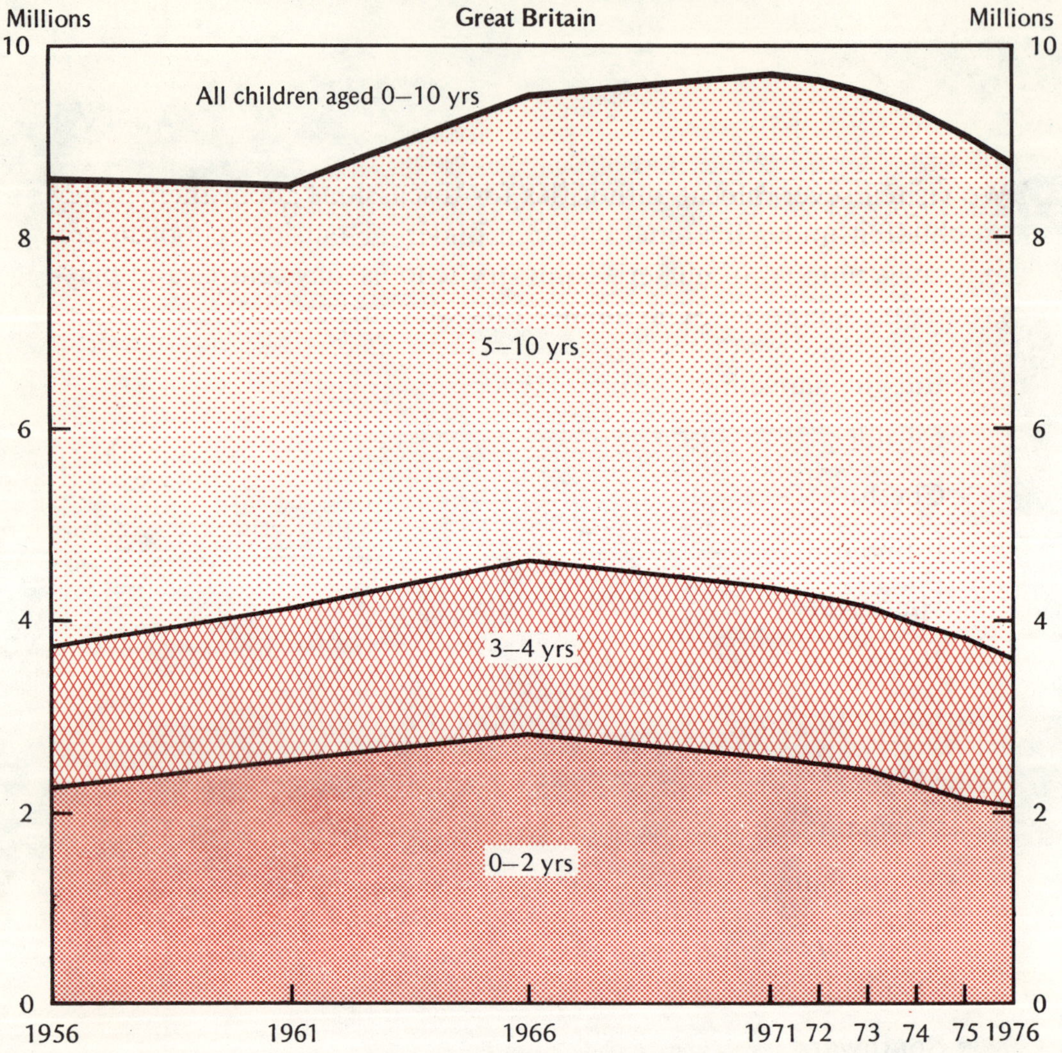

Millions
10

All children aged 0–10 yrs

5–10 yrs

3–4 yrs

0–2 yrs

8

6

4

2

0

Millions
10

8

6

4

2

0

1956   1961   1966   1971 72 73 74 75 1976

Geographical distribution of children aged 0–9, 1976
Great Britain

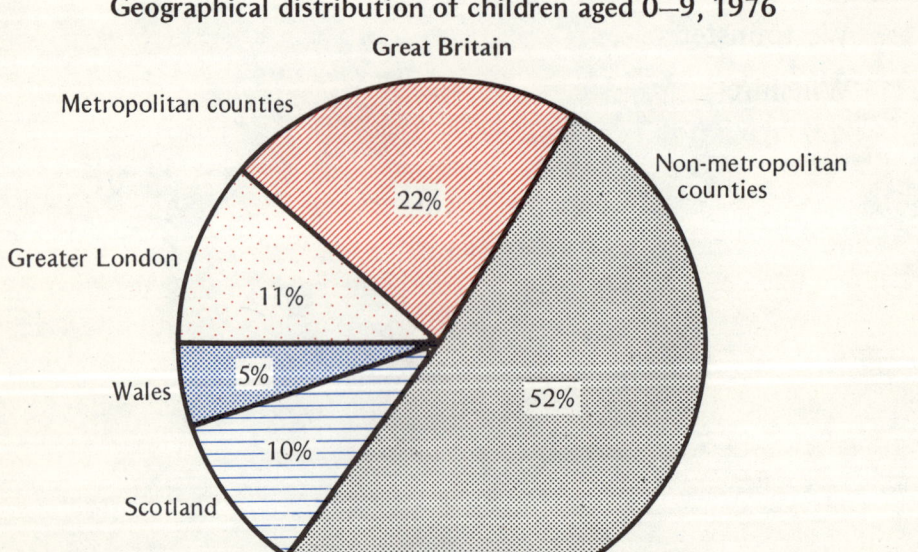

Metropolitan counties

Non-metropolitan counties

Greater London

Wales

Scotland

22%

11%

5%

10%

52%

DEMOGRAPHY AND EMPLOYMENT: PRESENT AND FUTURE TRENDS

1. There have been large changes in the child population in recent years. The number of children under 11 is now falling very sharply indeed, and the number of children under 5 has been falling for a decade. For example, the 3·6 million children under 5 in Great Britain in 1976 represented a drop of a million children in the age group over a decade earlier. Similarly the number of school children between 5 and 10, which rose steadily from 1961 to 1972 to a peak of 5·4 million, is now declining rapidly and will continue to do so until at least 1982–3. (Chart A shows the number of children under 11 since 1956.)

Geographical Distribution

2. The regional variations in the number of children are not substantial, though there are obviously significant local differences. The distribution of young children throughout the country broadly follows that of the population as a whole—the South East has the greatest number, East Anglia the lowest. In the same way, the share of young children living in conurbations (about one-third) is the same as of the total population. (Chart B shows the distribution of children under 10 throughout Great Britain.)

3. Looking at it another way the proportion that young children form of the total population is similar region by region. For example, the region with the smallest proportion of its population under 11 is the South West (15 per cent), and that with the highest is Scotland (17 per cent). Likewise, in most individual local authorities the proportion of the total population that are children is similar. Taking the under fives as an example, they form about 6 to 7 per cent of the population both in metropolitan districts and non-metropolitan counties. The inner London Boroughs are the exception, where the corresponding figure drops to around 4–6 per cent. Here the decline in the birth rate has been accentuated by population shifts among young families.

4. All these figures indicate that the sharp decline in the child population is not confined to any particular region. However, there are obviously some local authority areas, for example, new or expanding towns, which may have more than the normal share of young children. But apart from these exceptional areas, there is little evidence that any one area of the country has a greater need, on demographic grounds alone, for services for young children than another, whatever other factors there may be for giving priority to particular places.

Family Size

5. The traditional view of children and their families tends to assume the existence of the " normal " nuclear family of two parents and several children, with fairly clearly defined responsibilities for the upbringing of the children spread between the parents. But the structure of families in which young children are growing up is changing. In Great Britain for example, between 1971 and 1976 the proportion of children under 10 in family units with a single parent increased from 7 per cent to 9 per cent when the total number of children in the age group fell by 11 per cent. Families are also growing substantially smaller. For example in 1971 nearly 20 per cent of young children were in families of 4 or more children. By 1976 the percentage had fallen to 14 (Chart C).

Working Mothers

6. The proportion of working mothers with young children shows an upward trend. In Great Britain between 1961 and 1971 the proportion of mothers who had a child under five and who worked rose from 12 to 19 per cent. For those with a primary-school age child the increase was from 24 to 39 per cent. (*Table 1*.) It is estimated that by 1976 the proportion of mothers with children under five who worked had risen to about 25 per cent.

TABLE 1

The Percentage of Mothers with Children of Particular Ages who are in Employment
Great Britain

Mothers with children aged				1961	1966	1971
					Percentage	
0–4	...	...	...	11·5	17·2	18·7
5–10	...	...	...	24·3	33·4	38·5

Source: Census 10 per cent sample.

7. This increase obviously means a large proportion of young children now have mothers who work. The General Household Survey, has been used to estimate that in Great Britain in 1976 there were nearly 3·4 million children aged 0–10 whose mothers

Chart C

Dependent children aged 0–9 by size of family, 1971 and 1976
Great Britain

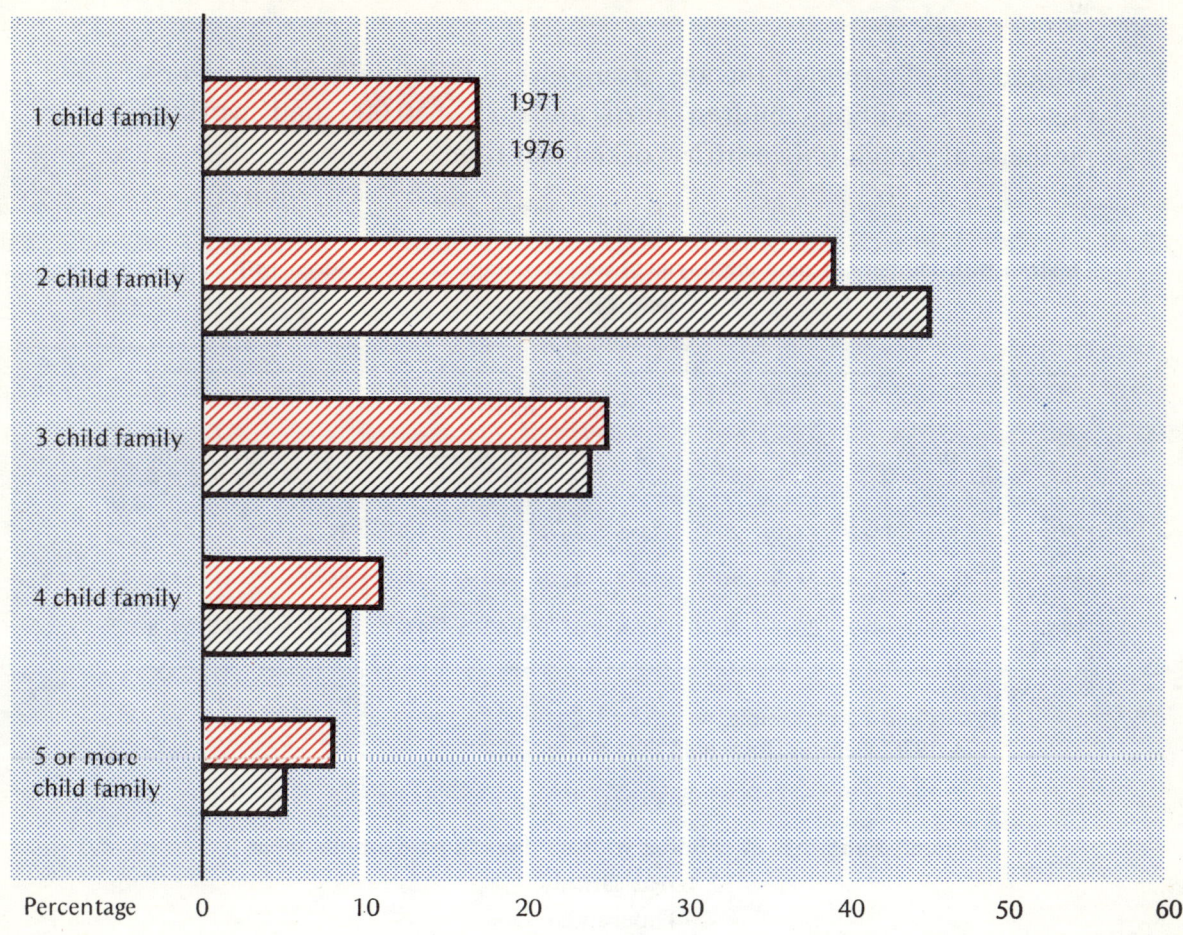

1 child family — 1971 / 1976

2 child family

3 child family

4 child family

5 or more child family

Percentage 0   10   20   30   40   50   60

Children of mothers in paid employment
As a percentage of all children with mothers
Great Britain

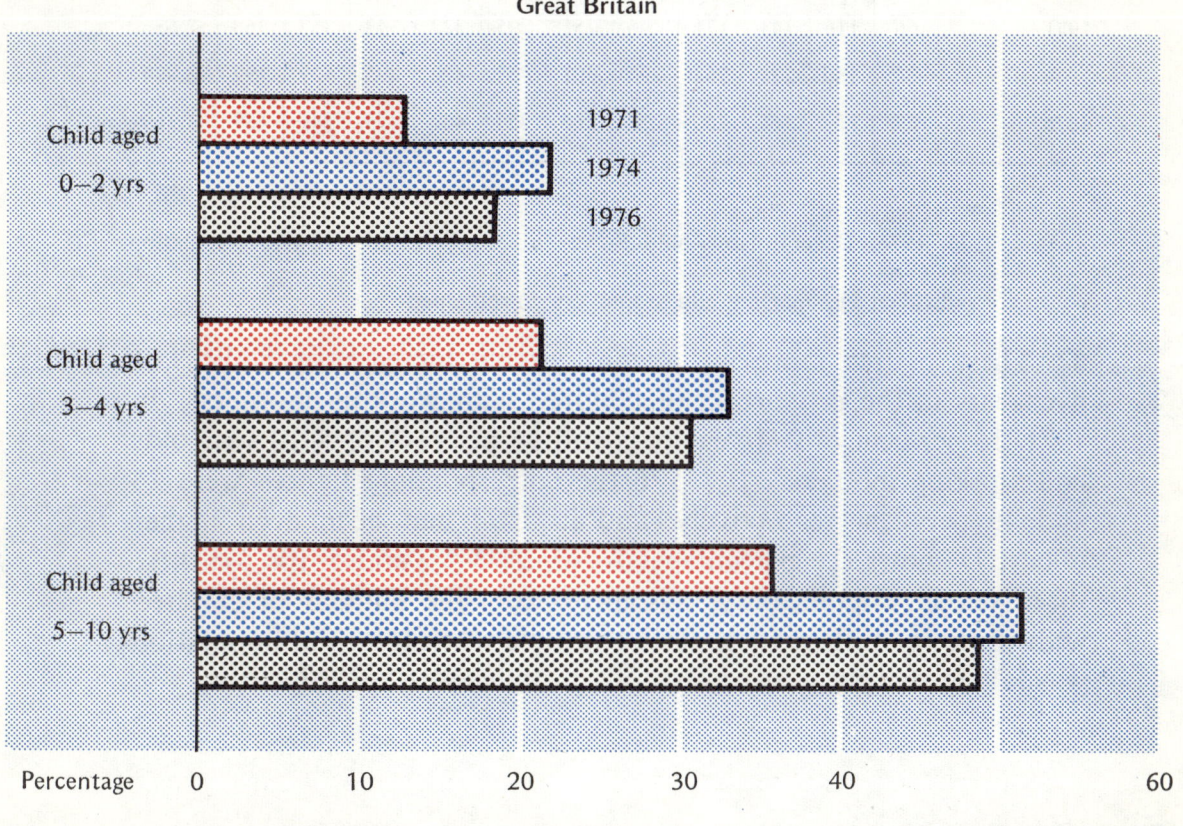

Child aged 0–2 yrs — 1971 / 1974 / 1976

Child aged 3–4 yrs

Child aged 5–10 yrs

Percentage 0   10   20   30   40   60

F

worked out of a total in the age group of 8·8 million (*Tables 2 and 3*). Out of 3·6 million children aged under 5, 850,000 had working mothers, although only a fifth worked full-time.

TABLE 2

Children with mothers in paid employment as percentage of all children with mothers
Great Britain
(Percentage)

						Age of child						
	0	1	2	3	4	5	6	7	8	9	10
1971 ...	8·2	14·2	17·0	20·2	23·5	28·6	33·0	36·5	39·8	42·1	44·7
1974 ...	11·8	23·6	28·9	30·6	35·3	43·9	49·6	47·1	55·2	57·4	54·2
1976 ...	11·8	18·9	23·3	26·4	34·4	43·0	42·5	47·1	53·1	50·4	54·8

Sources:
1971: Census 10% sample.
1974, 1976: General Household Survey.

TABLE 3

Estimated numbers of children with mothers in paid employment
Great Britain
(Thousands)

						Age of child							
	0	1	2	3	4	5	6	7	8	9	10	*Total 0–10
1971 ...	66	116	143	171	206	251	295	322	343	357	368	2,636
1974 ...	84	180	235	262	295	381	427	422	495	527	497	3,804
1976 ...	77	129	164	200	278	366	353	407	455	449	489	3,369

Sources:
1971: Census, 10% sample.
1974, 1976: General Household Survey rates applied to mid-year population estimates.
* Individual ages may not add to total due to rounding.

8. These figures represent a considerable increase over the last five years in the proportion of children with working mothers. In 1971, 16 per cent of 0–4 year olds and 36 per cent of 5–10 year olds had working mothers. By 1976 the corresponding figures were 24 and 49 per cent respectively, and in 1974 had been even higher (Chart D shows the percentages for 0–2s, 3–4s, and 5–10s for these three years). Significantly, this increase in the number of children with working mothers took place at a time when the child population was falling sharply.

Hours of Work

9. Although surprisingly large numbers of mothers with young children work, the number of hours they work for is obviously of considerable significance. The majority of mothers of young children in this country work for 30 hours or less per week (*Table 4*). Between 1971 and 1976 there was a shift towards working fewer hours although more women overall have jobs. Nevertheless in 1976 just over a quarter of children under three with working mothers had mothers who worked for more than 30 hours a week. This means that nearly 100,000 very young children had mothers who worked for a very substantial proportion of the working week. Perhaps slightly surprisingly, in the 3–4 age group a smaller proportion worked for more than 30 hours—16 per cent, or the mothers of 75,000 children (*Table 5*).

TABLE 4

Children of mothers in paid employment by age group of child and hours worked per week

Great Britain

(Percentages)

Year and age of child	All children with mothers in paid employment*	Number of hours worked per week			
		0–12	13–21	22–30	Over 30
1971					
0–2 ...	100	22·7	29·0	12·5	30·4
3–4 ...	100	22·4	30·7	14·4	28·1
5–10 ...	100	18·1	28·5	20·2	29·4
1974					
0–2 ...	100	36·8	31·2	13·0	17·9
3–4 ...	100	31·3	31·3	18·7	18·4
5–10 ...	100	23·3	30·7	21·0	24·4
1976					
0–2 ...	100	38·2	21·8	11·6	26·2
3–4 ...	100	34·5	32·3	15·7	15·7
5–10 ...	100	23·9	29·5	22·2	23·4

* Percentages do not add to 100% as mothers not stating number of hours worked are excluded from the table.

Sources:

1971: Census, 10% sample.

1974, 1976: General Household Survey.

TABLE 5

**Children of mothers in paid employment by age group of child and
hours worked**

Great Britain

(Thousands)

Year and age of child	All children with mothers in paid employment*	Number of hours worked per week			
		0–12	13–21	22–30	Over 30
1971					
0–2 ...	325	74	94	41	99
3–4 ...	376	84	115	54	106
5–10 ...	1,935	350	552	391	569
1974					
0–2 ...	499	184	156	65	89
3–4 ...	557	174	174	104	103
5–10 ...	2,748	640	844	577	671
1976					
0–2 ...	370	141	81	43	97
3–4 ...	479	165	155	75	75
5–10 ...	2,520	602	744	560	590

* Groups will not add to total as mothers not stating number of hours worked
are excluded from the table.

Sources :

    1971: Census, 10% sample.

    1974, 1976: General Household Survey rates applied to mid-year
population estimates.

School Age Children

10. Children between the ages of 5 and 10 are of course of
statutory school age and the employment figures suggest that it
may be easier for their mothers to work even though the children
are only occupied between 9.00 and 3.30 for approximately 39
weeks of the year. In 1976 for example there were nearly 600,000
children between 5 and 10 whose mothers worked for more than 30
hours, and a further 560,000 whose mothers worked between 22 and
30 hours a week.

Employment

11. The employment that is undertaken by the mothers of young
children is obviously highly dependent on the kind of job which
is available near their home and the social conventions which affect

the work that women do in their local area. For example, in some areas there is a strong tradition for married women to work, particularly in the textile and clothing industries. However, over 70 per cent of all working married women in this country worked in the service sector in 1975. The service sector is probably more likely to be able to provide part time employment of the kind most suitable for mothers with young children—night work, daytime shift work and work in schools which can be tied in with the demands of school holidays.

12. In general women are more likely to work part time when they are in the peak childbearing years. In 1975, of the total numbers of married women between the ages of 20 and 24 who were working, nearly 80 per cent worked for over 30 hours, but of the 25–34 year olds only 45 per cent of the total worked for over 30 hours.

13. The care of children imposes certain restrictions on the kind and amount of work which can be undertaken by mothers. They are far more likely to work in the lower paid service industries rather than in manufacturing. They are much more likely to work part-time and they are also likely to be extremely vulnerable to changes in the local economic climate.

14. While it is possible to obtain quite detailed information on how many hours women work, it is very difficult to tell *when* the hours are worked—or where. One study[1] has concluded tentatively that where mothers do work, about half work on five days a week and perhaps a tenth to a fifth work on six or seven days, leaving a substantial minority working on less than five days in any week.

15. The times at which work is done in the day are very difficult to establish. A study in 1968[2] suggested that as many as 59 per cent of women with children of school age or less work variable hours of no set pattern. A more recent study carried out in 1974[3] suggested that family arrangements were still the most significant form of care for young children. This reflects the extent to which women work when other members of their family are at home to look after the children—particularly presumably in the evenings, at weekends and overnight.

Future Trends
16. The information available about working mothers and their children in the recent past shows that there has been an increase in

[1] Mothers in Employment: Fonda & Moss 1976.
[2] Families and their Needs: HMSO 1968.
[3] Pre-school Children and their Need for Day Care. Margaret Bone: OPCS 1977.

the numbers of children under 11 with working mothers in the last twenty-five years. The question of how those trends will continue over the future years is obviously impossible to answer other than by a series of informed guesses.

The future birth rate

17. The birth rate has been declining steeply since 1964 following a steady upward trend in the previous ten years. It is now at its lowest level this century. Whether the fall will continue is difficult to predict. The decline is in line with long term movements in Europe and other advanced countries towards reduced family size, but this underlying trend may have been reinforced in recent years in this country by a general tendency to defer child bearing from the early years of marriage; this might explain the exceptionally steep decline in recent years. If this is so, the decline may be a temporary one.

18. But unless the rate continues to drop to a startling degree the absolute numbers of children born should begin to rise in the next few years as the girls born in the late 1950s and early 1960s reach child-bearing age. Chart E shows population projections for children to 1991 based on three variants which reflect the uncertainty of the future trend. Even if the high variant is discounted, the figures show that for as early a year as 1982 (for which planning should be taking place now) the variation in numbers of under three year olds could be as wide as 200,000.

19. The other significant aspect of these projections is the year by year variation which could be substantial. Provision of services has to be extremely flexible to cope with variations in demand for, say, primary education, of one-fifth over a twenty-five year period. Similarly, the provision of health and welfare services for children below school age may have to deal with similar numbers of children in 1976 and 1986 but with a substantial drop in numbers in between.

Future Employment Patterns

20. It is difficult to predict the future pattern of employment for mothers. Between June 1974 and June 1977, the number of male employees in employment is estimated to have fallen by 270,000 while female employment has increased by about 150,000 over the same period. This may reflect the heavy concentration of women employees in the service industries which are less immediately susceptible to the effects of the recession and to structural problems of the sort besetting manufacturing industry. If male unemployment

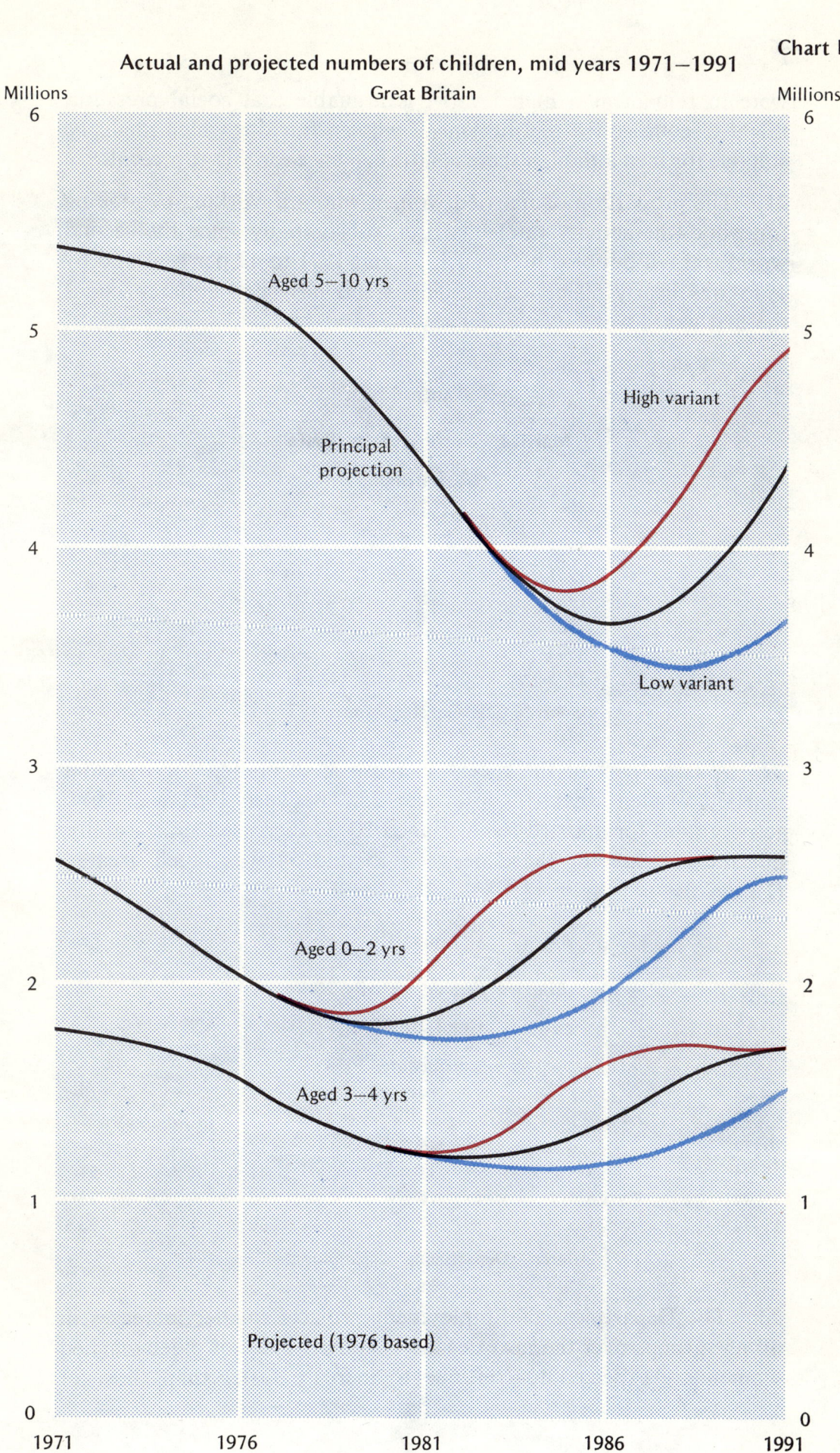

Actual and projected numbers of children, mid years 1971–1991   Chart E

Great Britain

Millions   Millions

Aged 5–10 yrs

Principal
projection

High variant

Low variant

Aged 0–2 yrs

Aged 3–4 yrs

Projected (1976 based)

1971   1976   1981   1986   1991

were to remain at a high level it is arguable that social pressures might discourage the recruitment of women for jobs which might be suitable for men although there is little evidence for this at present.

21.   The proportion of married women who are working or looking for work (the activity rate) has risen substantially since the second world war—it doubled between 1951 and 1971 to 42 per cent and by 1975 was nearly 50 per cent.   This trend has been apparent since the first world war.   (*Table 6.*)

TABLE 6

Married Female Activity Rates

Great Britain

	%
1921	8·7
1931	10·0
1951	21·7
1961	29·7
1971	42·3
1975	47·9

Source : DE Gazette: June, 1977.

22.   A large part of the recent increase is accounted for by older married women; that is, those over 35.   Between 1961 and 1971, activity rates for married females aged 20–34 increased substantially, but the increase for those between 35 and 54 was much greater. (*Table 7.*)

TABLE 7

Married Female Activity Rates

Great Britain

Percentage

Age	1961	1971	1976	1986
				(*estimated*)
20–24	41·4	46·7	54·6	55·7
25–34	29·5	38·4	47·8	51·5
35–44	36·4	54·5	66·4	73·8
45–54	35·3	57·0	66·3	76·0

Source : Department of Employment

23.   The Department of Employment projects smaller increases in all age-groups over the next decade.   Activity rates of older married women are expected to continue to increase faster than those of younger women. However, this assumes, inter alia, that the currently projected up-turn in the birth-rate may affect activity rates of women in the younger age groups.

24. For the future, it seems reasonable to assume that the proportion of mothers—including those with very young children—who are economically active will continue to increase. The assumption underlying current population projections is of an up-turn in the birth rate in the next few years. Considerable uncertainty surrounds both these assumptions, but, taken together, they could indicate an increase in the number of children needing day-care provision. However this will also depend on future growth in employment opportunities for married women.

EXISTING SERVICES FOR YOUNG CHILDREN AND THEIR FAMILIES

Full-time day care

1. Parents who need full-time day care for their children may go to a number of different agencies for it; local authority social service departments and, in some areas, voluntary societies, run full-time day nurseries which provide day care for children between the hours of about 7.30 a.m. and 6 p.m. In addition there are private day nurseries run on similar lines to those of the local authorities, employers' nurseries, creches, and childminders who work in their own home and are paid directly by the parents using them. In addition there have been some recent developments in the use of day fostering by local authorities who either pay a childminder's fee or have salaried childminders providing day care in their own homes under closer supervision from the local authority social services department.

Day nurseries

2. In 1976 local authorities in Great Britain provided 30,500 full time and 4,700 part time day nursery places for children under 5. The proportion of places to the child population varies widely from local authority area to area and depends to a large extent on the importance attached to the service by the local authority concerned. The ratio which is advised by DHSS for day nurseries is 8 places per thousand child population under the age of 5, so that the national figures represent adequate provision provided the ratio set by DHSS is a realistic and reasonable one. However, this ratio is at best merely a guide and does not appear to represent any scientific estimate of the extent of need. Furthermore, the national figures obviously mask very wide differences in local authority provision from those local authorities who provide twice or three times the recommended number to those who make no provision whatever for day nurseries (Annex 5 sets out the numbers of day nursery places and the rate per 1000 in the under fives population for all local authorities in Great Britain).

3. Local authority day nurseries are run by a matron and a staff—most are trained for the National Nursery Education Board certificate for nursery nurses. The ratio of staff to children is about 1 to

5 or 6 although the ratio may appear higher where there are a number of trainee nurses working. The training is a two year further education course dealing to a very large extent with child development which is undertaken by girls of 16 immediately they leave school.

4. Places in day nurseries are strictly controlled. A child can generally only get a place in a day nursery after a recommendation has been made by a social worker and the case has been considered by a committee consisting of the social worker, health visitor and the nursery matron concerned, even where the needs of the child or its family for a place at the day nursery are extremely pressing. In many areas the shortage of places is such that it is impossible to find a place rapidly even for a child in real need. The greater professional awareness of the problems of child abuse in recent years has meant that top priority for nursery places is given to children who are 'at risk' or who are thought to have already been damaged by their parents; children with unsatisfactory home backgrounds and in particular with unsatisfactory housing conditions are also given some priority as are the children of single parent families where their parent is anxious and able to return to work.

5. The evidence of the high rate of demand for day nursery places is clear from DHSS statistics which indicate that there are at any one time waiting lists of up to 12,000 children for places at full-time day nurseries in England. Many of these children will of course reach statutory school age before a place can be found for them. The waiting lists, although they are often out of date and only represent a proportion of need are sufficiently large to suggest that the DHSS assessment of a reasonable average ratio of places to the child population is no longer a realistic one and needs urgent revision.

6. Day nurseries are increasingly becoming institutions for dealing with children who are undergoing some kind of serious crisis or for dealing with long term needs which cannot be met by parents. This change has affected the kind of job that the nurseries have to do. In many cases they now cope primarily with children in need of intensive care and support and in most cases they also deal directly and closely with parents whose needs are equally great. The training, organisation and routine of day nurseries are still geared to dealing with fairly normal children whose parents are at work—the traditional role of the day nursery. The change in recent years to providing intensive support for children and their families frequently as an intermediary for the social service departments has meant that the staff of day nurseries can be under a severe strain with which in many cases they find it difficult to cope.

7. The cost of day nursery provision is high. In November 1975 the capital cost of a place was £3,400 and the revenue cost was £937 a year. In November 1976 the cost had risen to £3,800 and £1,130. Parents are normally charged a fee for a place at a day nursery; this is subject to a means test but a high proportion of the parents are very poor so that in most cases now the charge is nominal or non-existent.

8. Facilities in day nurseries vary enormously. Some are in modern purpose-built buildings which are light, airy and well equipped. Others are crammed into small converted flats or war-time nissen huts. However, there is no obvious correlation, to the external observer, between the standard of care given to the children and the kind of surroundings in which they spend their time. One of the most impressive things about all the nurseries we visited was the dedication shown by the staff. Even in the most unpropitious circumstances day nurseries were generally cheerful places and the staff were friendly and deeply concerned for the welfare of the children they were responsible for and their families.

Private Day Nurseries

9. Some areas of the country have private day nurseries, which provide a similar kind of care to that of the local authority day nursery but frequently to a lower standard both in terms of the ratio of staff to children and the equipment and physical surroundings. In 1976 there were 934 private nurseries in England, including those provided by employers, which could provide full-time day care for 26,000 children. The nurseries tend to be concentrated in those areas of the country where there is a tradition of skilled female employment and reasonably high wage levels. Thus in 1976 there were 72 day nurseries in the West Midlands, 205 in London (the highest number) and only 47 in the South West.

10. The fees at day nurseries can be fairly high, varying from £13 to £20 a week in 1977, and a number have had to close recently, partly because the cost of running a nursery has risen substantially in recent years and many parents are not able to meet higher fees.

Employers' Nurseries

11. Some firms provide nurseries, or crèches, for their employees. These provide day care for children below school age, normally only for the children of women working with the company. A small fee, usually heavily subsidised, is charged to the parent. In 1976 this was around £4 or £5 a week. This kind of provision is most likely to be valuable to those employers who have a skilled female labour force whose training is expensive, or in times of labour scarcity, when it is worthwhile subsidising a day nursery to retain experienced work-people.

Childminding

12. Most parents needing day care for their children who cannot claim any of the priority places in local authority nurseries take their children to childminders. Childminding has been established for a very long time and there has been statutory provision for some form of regulation of childminders since 1948. The basis of the system is that a parent agrees with a childminder to pay a fee in return for having the child looked after in the childminder's home for a proportion, or the whole, of a day. Inevitably the quality of child-minding varies enormously from person to person. In very recent years there has been a greater concentration on developing the role of childminders and encouraging them to do more with the children in their care than simply ensure that the children are reasonably fed and reasonably warm. This development work is normally carried out by the local authority but the extent of the local authority's involvement with childminders in its area depends entirely on the importance attached to childminding by the local authority.

13. In 1976 there were 83,000 permitted places for children with 31,000 registered childminders in England. In Scotland there were 1,012 places and in Wales there were 1,177. Annex 5 sets out the number of places and the rate per 1,000 children under five with registered childminders for each local authority in Great Britain.

14. Childminding provides more than twice as many places for children as local authority day nurseries but these numbers obviously only cover those childminders who are registered. The registration procedures, laid down for the first time by the 1948 childminding regulations, require the local authority to carry out fairly elementary checks on the health of the childminders, their record, and the safety and suitability of their home. Some local authorities attach a great deal of importance to registering childminders in their area and will ensure that a reasonably high proportion of childminding is carried on by registered childminders. In addition there may be modest incentives for childminders to register by, for example, running discussion groups and providing toys and training courses for the childminders who come forward for registration.

15. Nevertheless, it seems likely that the numbers of unregistered childminders are still very high. There are of course difficult border-line cases of children who are looked after by relations who may or may not be receiving money for doing so, and those who are merely ' helping out ' for a brief period. Some estimates of unregistered childminding run as high as 300,000, others are no more than 100,000. In many cases childminders do not register because they fail to realise that they need to do so or because they are frightened of being refused registration. In general local authorities tend to prefer to register a somewhat unsatisfactory minder than run the risk of an unregistered minder operating with no control whatever. Registration does give the local authorities the power to monitor the activities of the childminder and require some improvements to be made where they are necessary, whereas the normal consequence of deregistration is illegal childminding.

16. Childminding has received a lot of very critical publicity, mainly as a result of scandals concerning particular cases of neglect. Parents tend to prefer institutional care for their children rather than childminders unless they have found a good childminder. The success of the arrangement depends on the relationship between the parents, childminder and the child and in many cases children are moved from one childminder to another in an attempt to find the right kind of care, but with increasing problems for the child concerned.

17. Another major difficulty in the relationship between parents and childminders is money. Childminders on the whole tend to charge what they think the market will bear—in 1977 it was between £7 and £10 a week for a 5 day week. This could represent a very substantial sum for parents earning low wages but also give the childminder very little profit after meeting her expenses. In one recent study of childminding in London[1] a survey drew attention to the concern frequently expressed by both childminders and parents about the financial aspects of childminding.

18. Local authorities can do a considerable amount to improve the standard of childminding. The work of the National Children's Centre in Huddersfield has drawn attention to the advantages of training childminders and organising them into local groups to encourage them to provide facilities for the children in their care and to develop their skills in working with children. Some local authorities provide discussions on child care and development, give

[1] Childminding in London: London Council of Social Services 1977

advice and guidance on the day to day problems, provide toy libraries, encourage the development of discussion groups and the use of local facilities such as libraries, clinics, nursery schools and playgroups. All these resources contribute both to improving the standard of care for the children concerned and to encouraging the childminders to regard their job as being more than simply ' minding ' the children.

19. The extent of unregistered childminding must be a source of embarrassment and concern to some local authorities. There is a tendency to regard childminders as a convenient reservoir of labour to cope with the vast unsatisfied demand for child care which can be tapped at comparatively little cost to the government. It is probably the case that a large number of childminders undertake childminding only for a short period of time rather than as a professional career, to bring them in some money while they are tied to the house by their own small children. Nevertheless the damage that can be done by an unsuitable childminder is often very great and in areas where there is an acute shortage of childminders it is difficult for desperate parents to do much to control the standard of care that is provided for their children. Furthermore, if, as must frequently be the case, the childminder is unregistered there is little chance of the children in their care receiving the facilities which are available in health clinics, playgroups and through health visitors. The advantages and disadvantages of childminders are difficult to balance. A good childminder can provide a child with care which is frequently far better than that which the child could get at home but ' good ' childminders are rare, and difficult to find. Many parents will go to anyone apparently prepared to look after the child. The luxury of ' good ' care is one, for which few can afford to wait.

Part time Services

Nursery Schools and Classes

20. Nursery schools and classes can be provided by English local education authorities under the 1944 Education Act. There was a fairly rapid expansion of nursery education in the two years following the Conservative Government White Paper ' Education—A Framework for Expansion ' in 1972 but the more recent public expenditure cutbacks have hit the expansion of the nursery programme considerably. In most areas there has been no growth at all and such growth as there is most evident in big cities where the needs of deprived communities are most clearly to be seen. In January 1977 in England there were places in nursery schools and classes for 194,000 children under five and there were a further 245,000 children —of whom 143,000 were rising five—in ordinary classes in primary schools; of all these children about 175,000 were at school part-time for a half day session normally of between 2 and 3 hours. Nursery classes are normally run by a nursery teacher with a teacher training qualification assisted by nursery nurses with an NNEB qualification. The DES guidelines suggest a ratio of one teacher to 26 children and an overall ratio of one adult to 13 children.

21. In Scotland, nursery education is provided by local education authorities under the Education (Scotland) Act 1962. In 1972 a Scottish White Paper was published 'Education Scotland: A Statement of Policy' which sets out guidelines for education policy. The nursery classes in Scotland, as in England, are normally in the charge of a nursery teacher. The guidance on staffing ratios for Scotland ensures a ratio of one adult to 10 children, the teacher : pupil ratio varying from 1 : 20 to 1 : 40 as the number of places increases.

22. Nursery provision is not mandatory and is therefore often regarded as unnecessary or unimportant by the local education committee. The pattern of provision therefore tends to reflect local political prejudices as much if not more than local needs; an area of traditional concern for children under school age will frequently have a flourishing and adventurous nursery education sector while some areas make virtually no provision at all. Annex 5 sets out the numbers of full and part time places and the rates per 1000 children under five for all local authorities in Great Britain.

23. In those areas of the country where nursery education is being developed there are a large number of interesting experiments under way to use the nursery school as a means not only of developing the child in its early years but also to provide help, support, encouragement and education to parents. In many areas the head teacher in a nursery school class frequently finds herself performing the same kind of advisory role with parents as that provided by a matron in a day nursery. The teacher is often the first official person with whom parents have any kind of regular contact and is the one to whom they therefore turn for advice and help. Some teachers, particularly those in areas with a high concentration of deprivation find that they can spend a substantial proportion of their time counselling parents both in situations of acute crisis as well as in day to day discussion about the care and development of the children.

Private Nursery Schools

24. In some parts of the country there are also private nursery schools providing a wide variety of pre-school experience for small children. Some are the lineal descendants of the Dame's schools in a front room, while others follow a carefully planned system of child development. A few will even provide uniformed 3 year olds with something approaching a ' formal ' education.

Playgroups

25. Playgroups normally provide part-time sessions of 2 to 3 hours, in the mornings or afternoons during which the children take part in various activities under the guidance either, of a teacher, a play-group worker, or their parents. In general, playgroups are designed to encourage the development of the child, although a few local authorities are developing them as a means of support for parents as well. The main provider of part-time care—the playgroups which are members of the Pre-School Playgroups Association, are committed to the development of the child by working with both parents and children and involving the parents not only in the activities within the playgroup but in the organisation and running of it.

26. The playgroup movement has been in existence for some 15 years. If a group is part of the Pre-school Playgroups Association (PPA) it is normally organised as a small local group run by the parents who provide the staff from among themselves. In Scotland the Scottish Pre-school Playgroups Association, and in Wales the Welsh language playgroups run by Mudiad Ysgolion Meithrin are organised on similar lines. The Association has grown phenomenally, particularly in the last decade. In 1976 there were over 400,000 children in playgroups in Great Britain. The playgroups provide anything from 1 or 2 to 5 sessions a week for each child and charge a fee, which ranged from 15p to 50p a session in 1977. They receive some help from the social services department of local authorities who are responsible for registering them under the childminding regulations but the amount of assistance varies widely from place to place and will normally depend on the importance attached to the development of services for the under-fives by the local authority. In addition some local authorities will sponsor a certain number of places at playgroups for children who they think need the benefits of the playgroup but whose parents cannot afford the fees. Annex 5 sets out the number of places in playgroups and the rate per 1000 children under five for all local authorities in Great Britain.

27. In addition to the work done by the PPA, the term ' playgroup ' is increasingly being used to cover various experimental forms of day care for children between 3 and 5. Some local authorities have set up their own playgroups which are run by their own salaried workers and are really a form of part time professional day care rather than playgroups in the classic PPA sense. In addition the voluntary societies run playgroups in areas of particular deprivation but they again are normally designed to provide care for the children, and in some cases support for the parents, in a rather different way from the parental involvement in the Playgroup Movement's groups.

28. The registration and inspection of playgroups are primarily the responsibility of local authority social service departments. Nevertheless they provide a service for the same age group as nursery schools and classes which come under the auspices of the local authority education department. Difficulties can arise where the two forms of provision appear to be competing with each other. The PPA philosophy stresses the joint development of the child and parents together. The nursery school tends to emphasize the development of the child as an individual and its preparation for school. Where both nursery classes and playgroups are available parents tend to opt for the more traditional nursery class form of care for their children, partly because they are more used to the less demanding requirements for them of the educational system, because nursery classes are free and because the transition from nursery class to school, particularly if they are part of the same institution, is easier for the children. Where there is very close co-ordination between playgroups and schools both can flourish, and of course those areas of the country where there are enough nursery and playgroup places to meet demand are few and far between. It is far more usual to find nursery classes with long waiting lists having close contacts with local playgroups because of the shortage of places and directing parents to their local playgroup because there is no chance of their child having a place in a nursery class.

Advisory Services

29. Advice to parents about the health and development of their children comes primarily from the medical services assisting at the birth of the child, and their family doctor and the health visitor responsible for the child after its birth. In 1976 there were nearly 9,000 health visitors in Great Britain who paid slightly over 700,000 visits to children under a year old and 2 million visits to other children under the age of 5. Their major task is to advise and support the parents during the early years of the child's life, and to observe the development of the child and step in with advice and help where this seems to be necessary. Health visitors are trained nurses who have done an additional professional training. They have other responsibilities particularly for the elderly, (to whom they paid 670,000 visits in Great Britain in 1976) but the majority of their time is spent on visiting families with young children.

30. In addition to the domiciliary visiting by health visitors parents can also obtain advice and help about the health and development of their children from clinics run normally by health visitors or GPs or from their own doctor. In 1976 in Great Britain 1·7 million children below the age of 5 attended child health clinics out of a total of 3·6 million in the age group.

31. All these forms of professional advice go some way to helping with one of the growing problems for parents with young children— the high rate of depressive illnesses and isolation among mothers at home. In recent years there has been some development of rather more informal ways of coping with the needs of mothers with young children in particular for companionship and an escape from their own home. A number of local authorities and their organisations run " mother and toddler " clubs whose apparent purpose is to provide a place where very small children can play supervised by their parents but which in fact tend to perform an important thera-peutic role for the mothers in providing them with companionship of people in similar circumstances to their own and, where there is some kind of organiser or play leader, with a source of advice and help which is not immediately connected with the normal establish-ment of professional advisers. The distribution of this kind of informal support is obviously variable and can often depend as much on the availability of resources within the Parks department of a local authority to provide the necessary facilities as on any perception of need by the Social Services departments.

THE ADMINISTRATION OF SERVICES FOR CHILDREN

1. The pattern of services for children at a local level is broadly the same in England, Wales, and Scotland. The main difference is in the administration of policy centrally. In England it is divided between the Department of Health and Social Security and the Department of Education and Science; in Scotland, it is the responsibility of the Scottish Office, although the services in Scotland operate under different legislation, and in Wales of the Welsh Office.

England

The Department of Health and Social Security

2. The Department gives guidance to the local authorities who have responsibilities for day care facilities for children under the various Acts of Parliament providing for the supervision and control of the care of young children. The Department provides loan sanction for capital projects in their Local Authority Social Services Division. There is technical and professional support from social work-trained advisers, the medical and the nursing divisions.

3. Policy development for the personal social services dealing with children are the responsibility of the branches coming within Children's Division. These are divided into four, dealing with delinquency, children at risk, children's health and adoption. Physically and mentally handicapped children are not dealt with in the Children's Divisions but are the concern of the specialist divisions responsible for health and mental health. Health services in general are covered by a separate division.

4. The Department's Social Work Service operates on a regional basis throughout the country, and provides a link between the department's headquarters and the local authorities. The Social Work Service consists of trained social workers who act as Advisers to the Department. The Department also sends out circulars and letters to the local authorities giving advice and exhortation. The last two circulars which have been sent out on policy for under fives have been jointly circulated with the Department of Education and Science.

5. The area in which DHSS is most able to take direct steps is that of encouraging the voluntary organisations. There are a large number of voluntary organisations dealing with needs of children ranging from the extremely large national organisations to small local groups. DHSS discusses the work of voluntary associations with them and will make grants to them to cover the cost of their national organisation but will not give grants to them to cover the provision of local services—these are the responsibility of the local authorities. The Department makes grants of about £5 million each year to the voluntary societies generally. The expenditure usually covers research projects, administrative expenses and training programmes.

Local Authority Social Service Departments

6. The Social Service departments have a number of statutory responsibilities for children. They are required to provide day care facilities for children " who have not obtained the age of 5 years and are not attending primary schools maintained by a local education authority " under Section 21 of the National Health Service Act 1977.

7. Section 1 of the Children and Young Person's Act 1973 lays on local authorities a duty to make available " such advice, guidance and assistance as may promote the welfare of children by diminishing the need to receive children into or keep them in care ". This is a general power under which local authorities help parents to meet the cost of day care charges and the cost of transport or play group charges where this is necessary. It is a somewhat curiously worded provision and could be interpreted as laying a statutory duty on local authorities to do far more in the area of advice and assistance for children than is the case at the present moment. It is, however, sufficiently wide to enable those local authorities who wish to do so to undertake a certain amount of experimentation in the whole field of advisory services for children's welfare.

8. Local authorities' responsibilities for the day care facilities for children provided by private individuals are imposed by the Nurseries and Childminders Regulation Act 1948 and the Health Services and Public Health Act 1968. All private provision of facilities for children including day nurseries, childminding and play groups have to be registered with the social service department which is empowered to lay down requirements to ensure the welfare and health of the children to be looked after.

9. Most local authorities carry out their responsibilities under the 1968 Act by inspecting the premises of anyone who applies for registration and in many cases by generally overseeing those registered in order to ensure the maintenance of standards. In addition, local authorities in some areas provide advisory services for childminders and playgroups although the provision of these additional services varies very widely from one local authority to another.

10. Local authorities also work with voluntary associations, normally by means of grant-aiding to assist them in setting up, playgroups or day nurseries. They may help with advice or provision of equipment or premises and frequently sponsor places for children they consider to be in need of the services provided by the voluntary association.

Department of Education and Science

11. The Department of Education and Science organises the nursery school programme under Section 8 of the 1944 Education Act. Annual expenditure on the nursery programme nationally is set by the Department who then agree to the allocation of resources for loan sanction for capital projects for particular local authorities. The main control exercised by DES is over the number of places which are provided in any area rather than on the specific details of particular building projects. This is in contrast to the system followed by DHSS who control in far greater detail the type and quality of provision made.

12. Unlike the organisation for primary and secondary education, nursery education in DES is not organised on a territorial basis but is all handled within a single branch. There is thus no immediate link between the provision of nursery education and the provision of primary and secondary education in any area although there is communication between the nursery education branch and the relevant territorial division when plans are being cleared. Nevertheless this must inevitably mean that nursery education is handled as a special case and not necessarily seen as an integrated part of the educational system of any area. It must also mean that the administrators responsible for nursery education and for the vetting of particular projects have less knowledge of the details of the areas with which they are concerned than would a territorial division looking at the provision of primary or secondary education.

13. In addition the Department has a programme of research on nursery education which is designed to cover all aspects of nursery education and will take some years to complete. They have a team of advisers on nursery education as part of the inspectors of schools who are linked with the inspectors who specialise in nursery education in each region of the country.

Local Education Authorities

14. Education authorities are empowered to provide nursery school provision under Section 8 of the 1944 Education Act. The first post war development in nursery education began in 1960 when a circular was issued which allowed local authorities to establish nursery classes where this enabled married women teachers to go out to work. In 1972 the White Paper "The Framework for Expansion" encouraged a far more rapid expansion in nursery education which lasted until the public expenditure cuts of 1975 caused severe cut backs in the programme. Local education authorities are free to decide whether or not they wish to provide nursery education and if they do, to a large extent the form in which it may be provided.

15. At the moment the falling numbers of school age children, which is affecting the size of infant schools, is encouraging those local authorities who wish to make nursery provision to make use of under-occupied primary school building, and set up nursery units within primary schools rather than separate nursery schools. The local authorities normally have an adviser who is responsible for overseeing the development of nursery education, who, in almost all instances, has had some experience teaching younger children.

16. The kind of staff available for nursery units varies widely. There is normally one trained teacher to every 30 children and an average of one adult to 10 to 13 children. The assistants are frequently NNEB trained nursery nurses.

The Professionals

17. There are a number of different professions who are involved with children under five and their parents. Most of them have a dual function which is already recognised, that of advising and helping parents and caring—in its widest sense—for the children. In general most professionals working with children accept that they have this role but many people argue that the training which is provided for all those working in this area does not yet fully accept that this is the case, and that most people starting work are inadequately prepared for the kind of demands which would be put upon them by parents as well as children.

Nursery Nurses

18. Nursery nurses receive a fairly basic training in child development and child care which lasts for two years and is normally undertaken by 16 year olds leaving school. It consists of a series of modules designed to cover amongst other things child development, nutrition, health and hygiene. At the end of the training an 18 year old can expect to know a reasonable amount of theory and to have had some supervised practical experience. The wastage rate of nursery nurses is high, its status and pay are low and the amount of subsequent in-service training is very small.

19. The one avenue of promotion for nursery nurses is to become a matron in a day nursery. There are some fairly short courses for matrons which have been cut back in recent months and many people who have taken the National Nursery Education Board certificate work in private nurseries or as private nannies. Others work as nursery assistants in nursery classes or nursery schools but they cannot progress any further without taking a teacher training qualification.

Teachers

20. Specialist courses for nursery teachers were abolished some years ago and combined courses for nursery and infant teachers were instituted instead. Some nursery teachers have been trained as teachers for infants dealing with the age group from 3–7. This development obviously makes it easier for teachers with nursery training and experience to widen their expertise in dealing with a range of age groups. It also ensures that they have greater access to opportunities for promotion than would be the case if they were trained only for nursery teaching. Nevertheless children entering school for the first time at the age of 3 do need some fairly specialist care, and the parental problems with which teachers of this age group are called upon to cope, are ones for which adequate training is obviously needed.

Health Visitors

21. The primary concern of health visitors is with the care and development of children in their very early years. They are state registered nurses with obstetric qualifications and a further one year's specialist training, and they see parents both in domiciliary visits and at clinics. They play an extremely important role in the education of parents in the care of children, and often act as an important bridge between the parents and the other social services which are available to them.

Scotland

22. Responsibility for services for children in Scotland are organised within the Scottish Office and, both the social work and education functions come within the ambit of the Scottish Education Department, whose staff include professional advisers on social work services and Her Majesty's Inspectors of Schools. This administrative amalgamation is not mirrored within local authorities where responsibility for such services is divided between the social work departments and the education departments in much the same way as in England. Nevertheless the closer liaison centrally is felt to help in the development of policies for young children.

23. The main Scottish legislation for children's services is the Social Work (Scotland) Act 1968, as amended, and the Education (Scotland) Act 1962, as amended, though the Nurseries and Childminders' Regulation Act 1948 also applies in Scotland. In 1972, there was a separate White Paper for Scotland " Education in Scotland: A Statement of Policy " which included the provision of services for children under 5. Like the two English Departments, the Scottish Education Department has certain responsibilities for local authority capital building programmes for services for chidren, and grants to voluntary organisations though the detailed arrangements may differ a little from those in England; there are also separate arrangements for the training of teachers and nursery nurses.

24. The general position on facilities for young children is broadly comparable in Scotland and England and also varies between local authority areas; there are several examples of imaginative projects, notably in the use of day nurseries as resource centres, but the overall pattern is one of under provision, in some areas very great need, and cut backs in expenditure in recent years. The figures of places for children under five per 1000 in the population in Scottish local authorities are in Annex 5.

Wales

25. Services for children in Wales are the responsibility of the Welsh Office in Cardiff and the local authorities. The Welsh Office gives advice on the provision of services to the local authorities. While responsibility for children can be more easily co-ordinated within the Welsh Office in Cardiff the local authorities follow the normal pattern of divided responsibility for social services and education services. Figures showing the number of places for children under five per 1000 in the population are in Annex 5.

Local authority area	Population under 5 at 30 June 1976	Places in:				Child (full-... par
		Local authority day nurseries		Private day nurseries		
		No.*	Rate per 1,000 under 5	No.	Rate per 1,000 under 5	No.
OUTER LONDON						
Barking	10,000	150	15·0	—	—	23
Barnet	18,700	239	12·8	44	2·4	34
Bexley	13,900	50	3·6	188	13·5	50
Brent	16,200	675	41·7	401	24·8	1,09
Bromley	17,700	50	2·8	173	9·8	71
Croydon	21,300	179	8·4	43	2·0	73
Ealing	19,700	353	17·9	80	4·1	1,10
Enfield	15,600	90	5·8	26	1·7	49
Haringey	15,100	280	18·5	155	10·3	49
Harrow	12,300	110	8·9	76	6·2	62
Havering	15,300	190	12·4	42	2·7	27
Hillingdon	14,100	200	14·2	42	3·0	19
Hounslow	12,200	174	14·3	406	33·3	38
Kingston-upon-Thames ...	8,000	96	12·0	121	15·1	60
Merton	9,400	139	14·8	152	16·2	35
Newham	16,600	225	13·6	76	4·6	1,91
Redbridge	13,300	100	7·5	241	18·1	35
Richmond-upon-Thames ...	9,000	135	15·0	140	15·6	58
Sutton	9,900	52	5·3	355	35·9	33
Waltham Forest	14,900	282	18·9	62	4·2	33
Total: OUTER LONDON ...	283,200	3,769	13·3	2,823	10·0	11,70
INNER LONDON						
Camden	7,700	742	96·4	417	54·2	17
Greenwich	12,800	125	9·8	34	2·7	6
Hackney	12,200	378	31·0	62	5·1	74
Hammersmith	9,900	498	50·3	104	10·5	50
Islington	9,800	604	61·6	179	18·3	36
Kensington	6,500	351	54·0	205	31·5	18
Lambeth	18,300	642	35·1	283	15·5	8
Lewisham	13,900	240	17·3	35	2·5	84
Southwark	12,100	516	42·6	—	—	50
Tower Hamlets	8,100	275	34·0	—	—	26
Wandsworth	17,400	418	24·0	491	28·2	8
Westminster	7,900	475	60·1	514	65·1	2
City of London	300	—	—	—	—	
Total: INNER LONDON ...	136,900	5,264	38·5	2,324	17·0	6,18

OR CHILDREN UNDER 5 : 1976

	31 March		Pupils in:									31 December
rs nd	Playgroups (part-time)		Nursery schools and classes (full-time) (excl. rising 5's)		Nursery schools and classes (part-time) (excl. rising 5's)		Nursery schools and classes (full-time and part-time) (Rising 5's only)		Non-nursery classes in primary schools (full-time and part-time) (excl. rising 5's)		Non-nursery classes in primary schools (full-time and part-time) (Rising 5's only)	
e per 000 er 5	No.	Rate per 1,000 under 5	No.	Rate per 1,000 under 5	No.	Rate per 1,000 under 5	No.	Rate per 1,000 under 5	No.	Rate per 1,000 under 5	No.	Rate per 1,000 under 5
3·8	1,004	100·4	286	28·6	312	31·2	83	8·3	606	60·6	462	46·2
8·3	2,519	134·7	235	12·6	1,129	60·4	5	0·3	1,169	62·5	819	43·8
6·5	2,362	169·9	26	1·9	428	30·8	50	3·6	131	9·4	537	38·6
7·7	1,524	94·1	297	18·3	761	47·0	2	0·1	1,095	67·6	770	47·5
0·3	4,233	9·2	22	1·2	85	4·8	6	0·3	281	15·9	632	35·7
4·6	3,227	151·5	210	9·9	211	9·9	37	1·7	1,005	47·2	986	46·3
6·0	1,750	88·8	114	5·8	1,305	66·2	2	0·1	1,299	65·9	967	49·1
1·9	2,026	129·9	14	0·9	757	48·5	2	0·1	889	57·0	827	53·0
2·5	764	50·6	274	18·1	1,373	90·9	6	0·4	1,001	66·3	681	45·1
0·7	1,932	157·1	101	8·2	424	34·5	1	0·1	175	14·2	660	53·7
8·2	2,216	144·8	3	0·2	215	14·1	40	2·6	801	52·4	797	52·1
4·0	1,869	132·6	25	1·8	1,314	93·2	27	1·9	923	65·5	747	53·0
1·3	1,071	87·8	27	2·2	1,077	88·3	18	1·5	926	75·9	637	52·2
6·0	791	98·9	89	11·1	805	100·6	14	1·8	322	40·3	409	51·1
7·7	1,001	106·5	53	5·6	1,064	113·2	11	1·2	524	55·7	477	50·7
5·2	1,222	73·6	83	5·0	2,235	134·6	108	6·5	127	7·7	577	34·8
6·9	3,278	246·5	14	1·1	442	33·2	53	4·0	85	6·4	519	39·0
4·8	1,930	214·4	55	6·1	251	27·9	27	3·0	579	64·3	366	40·7
4·2	1,467	148·2	82	8·3	472	47·7	124	12·5	1	0·1	35	3·5
2·5	2,097	140·7	61	4·1	1,019	68·4	37	2·5	439	29·5	620	41·6
1·3	38,283	135·2	2,071	7·3	15,679	55·4	653	2·3	12,378	43·7	12,525	44·2
2·1	1,168	151·7										
8·3	1,302	101·7										
1·0	938	76·9										
1·1	461	46·6										
7·0	1,066	108·8										
8·2	956	147·1										
8·0	2,014	110·1										
0·7	1,640	118·0										
2·0	1,521	125·7										
2·5	444	54·8										
1·4	1,814	104·3										
7·2	989	125·2										
—	18	60·0										
5·2	14,331	104·7	4,595	33·6	12,317	90·0	466	3·4	1,840	1·3	5,929	43·3

ANNEX 6

JOINT DES/DHSS CIRCULAR ON THE CO-ORDINATION OF PROVISION FOR THE UNDER-FIVES

Local Authority Social Services Letter LASSL(78)1

Health Notice HN(78)5

Department of Health and Social Security

Reference No: S47/24/013

Department of Education and Science

DEPARTMENT OF HEALTH AND SOCIAL SECURITY
DEPARTMENT OF EDUCATION AND SCIENCE

To:

Chief Executive,
    Non-Metropolitan County Councils
    Metropolitan District Councils
    London Borough Councils
    Common Council of the City of London

Education Officer, ILEA

Regional Health Authorities
Area Health Authorities

Copies to:
    Directors of Social Services
    Chief Education Officers
    Area Medical Officers (for Specialists in Community Medicine)
    Area Nursing Officers (for Area Nurse (Child Health))
    Community Health Councils

25 January 1978

Dear Sir

Co-ordination of Services for Children Under 5

1. This circular letter is issued jointly by the Department of Education and Science and Health and Social Security to reinforce their letter issued in March 1976 on the co-ordination of local authority services for children under five. The Departments recognise that resources available for the under fives are still far short of what is needed to make adequate provision for the group. The purpose of this letter is therefore to urge local authorities in general through co-ordination of all available services to make maximum use of existing resources in the education, social service and health fields provided by statutory authorities and also by the community itself through volunteers, or voluntary bodies. It invites those local authorities who are able to do so also to take full advantage of additional resources that may become available under the Inner Cities Programme, and the enlarged Urban Programme for 1978–79 in developing services for under fives. The provision of services for the under fives is a field in which the voluntary bodies have a permanent role : it is therefore important that they should be involved at every stage in the planning process.

2. The earlier circular letter concentrated on the machinery for co-ordination. This letter discusses ways in which better provision can be made as a result of co-ordination and provides examples in the Annex.

3. The response to the earlier letter has shown that there is already an encouraging measure of co-operation between authorities and agencies providing services for the under-fives. The growing co-operation between Education and Social Services Departments is a specially satisfactory feature of the reports that have been received. The Departments welcome these developments.

4. The Departments wish to record their appreciation of the valuable study " The Under-Fives " produced by the Local Authority Associations. This highlights matters for co-ordination at both national and local level and the Departments hope that this circular letter will complement the study's recommendations insofar as they can be acted upon at local level.

5. One of the recommendations of the study was that the legal impediments to the establishment of a joint committee for the under-fives with executive powers should be removed. This recommendation has been carefully considered but the Secretaries of State believe that a joint advisory committee responsible both to the Education Committee and the Social Services Committee offers a better way forward. Their view is based on the belief that joint committees for the under-fives with executive powers could cut across important existing links—for instance between nursery schools and primary schools, and between services for children and for families as a whole—with damaging effects.

6. At national level in addition to the inter-departmental meetings mentioned in paragraph 3 of the circular letter of 9 March 1976 and existing arrangements for consultation with local and health authorities, the two Departments propose to institute annual consultations with the Local Authority Associations and the voluntary bodies. In addition Ministers of the two Departments have themselves decided to meet regularly to review the progress made towards co-ordination of their Departments' activities as they affect under-fives.

The Need For Co-ordination

7. No services for young children and their families can operate in isolation; almost everyone working in this field has much to gain from the expertise and experience of people in other statutory, voluntary and community services. There is, therefore, a continuing need for the co-ordination of development plans and for arrangements to ensure contact and co-operation between all the agencies and authorities concerned. The Departments would also emphasise that services for children must be seen in the context of support for the family as a whole. They should complement and supplement, but not serve as a substitute for, paternal care. Parents' knowledge of, and concern for, the needs of their own children need building on, not replacing; furthermore, parents have a vital role to play in their involvement with the services provided by voluntary organisations and as a result of community initiatives. Research projects currently being carried out within the Departments' Research Programmes are specifically concerned with parental involvement.

Use of Resources

8. Restraints on national resources and the severe financial pressures on local authorities have inevitably affected expansion of nursery education and day nurseries provided for the under-fives. The Government remains committed to a continuing expansion of nursery education and to the development of day care services but recognises that for the majority of local authorities the pace of expansion must depend largely on resolving current economic problems. Over the next few years the resources that can be provided nationally will continue to be concentrated in areas of social and educational disadvantage and on recognising and meeting the needs of children socially, mentally or physically handicapped.

9. For many years some of the most deprived and decaying inner cities areas have become the first home of newly arrived immigrant groups and, because of poverty, ties with the family and the community, or other reasons, many have remained there. As a consequence many of the children of these groups have suffered from general social and environmental deprivations. Their disadvantage has been compounded by the problems arising from differences in language and culture. In providing services for disadvantaged children from ethnic minorities, local authorities should consider how their services and the way they are presented need to be modified to take account of linguistic and cultural differences. Advice can be obtained from the Centre for Information and Advice on Educational Disadvantage, 11 Anson Road, Manchester M14 5BY.

The Urban Programme

10. The White Paper " Policy for the Inner Cities " (Cmnd 6845) refers in paragraph 46 to the benefits for the under-fives which would derive from more effective co-ordination at the local level. The Departments therefore ask partnership authorities—and other authorities outside the partnership areas who are eligible to apply for grant aid under the provisions of paragraph 9 of the Department of the Environment Circular 122/77 (Urban Programme Circular 17) —to give consideration to the needs of the under-fives and in co-operation with voluntary organisations to formulate proposals for joint schemes to provide day care and education for children with a priority need.

11. Some authorities have appointed teachers to work with the under-fives as a way of extending the benefits of their professional skills to children for whom there is no nursery school or class in the area. The teachers, sometimes based on a nursery or infants school, work with children in their homes, with children in day nurseries or other forms of day care, with playgroups and in play buses or caravans. Authorities with areas eligible for grant under the urban programme will wish to consider the advantages of such arrangements.

Capital Expenditure

12. Both Departments currently operate building programmes which affect the under-fives. DES has a nursery education programme and invites local education authorities each year to put forward proposals for the expansion of nursery education provision preferably by adapting vacant primary schools space for use as nursery classes. Authorities are given lump sum allocations—DES does not approve individual projects. DHSS has a Personal Social Services programme, covering a wide range of provisions from day nurseries to homes for the elderly. Authorities propose projects in order of priority and DHSS approves individual projects, normally on the basis of the authorities' own priorities. In cases where an authority wishes to propose a scheme for the under fives, involving both education and care, which requires approval of capital expenditure both by DES and DHSS, the two Departments have arranged to consider such schemes jointly and a proportion of the cost will be set against the capital building programme of each Department. Local authorities putting forward joint projects should send them to both Departments making clear that they are for joint provision and indicating how they wish the cost to be shared between the Nursery Education and Personal Social Services Building Programmes, not necessarily in strict proportion to the respective education and social service elements. The Departments will not normally sanction a joint project to which an authority attaches low priority in its personal social services programme.

Education For The Under Fives

13. Nursery education is valuable for almost all children and should be especially helpful in compensating for the disadvantage suffered by children from socially and economically deprived homes. Parents suffering social and economic disadvantage including many in the ethnic minority groups, tend to a greater extent than others to use child-minders to provide day care for their children. While education should be an integral part of the care provided for children outside their homes, it is particularly important for children in the care of child-minders. These children should therefore be considered as having a high priority for the assistance provided by nursery teachers (see paragraph 11) or for the allocation of places in nursery schools and classes.

14. Nursery schools and classes provide a growing proportion of 3 and 4 year olds their first contact with the education system. The teaching staff are professionally qualified, equipment and materials are chosen for their educational value and the overriding objective is the child's linguistic, social, emotional and physical development. Parents are increasingly involved with teachers and children in the work of the nursery schools and classes.

15. Many children receiving day care do not attend such schools and classes and the Departments therefore hope that all authorities will examine the possibilities of improving the educational content

of the various forms of day care available in their areas. This could include the development of links between the education service and day centres and nurseries and playgroups as well as the special arrangements suggested for children in the care of child-minders in paragraph 13 above. The best way forward may be to take nursery education to the children by seeking to arrange for the nursery teachers to work directly with the children and those caring for them.

16. It is equally important that the desirability of linking the care, education and health services for the 3 and 4 year olds in areas of educational and social disadvantage should be recognised by authorities planning an expansion of nursery education so that these services are available for those children who need them most.

Day Nurseries

17. Day nurseries, some of which already operate as day centres, can serve as the focus for all day care services in their area, assisting in the improvement of the care provided elsewhere and helping to develop community services. One development which is recommended to authorities is the establishment of sponsored child-minding/day fostering schemes under the wing of day nurseries. These schemes are discussed more fully in paragraph 26 below, but attention is particularly drawn here to the way in which such schemes can help build closer links between day nursery staff and families living in the community they serve. Such links can also be developed between day nursery staff, nursery teachers, playgroups, mother and toddler groups and voluntary associations working with pre-school children in the local community to ensure that fullest use is made of the experience of staff working in the nursery, and to assist the staff themselves in becoming involved in the interests and life of the local community.

18. Increasingly, authorities are also recognising the educational needs of children who attend day nurseries and in some areas teachers are visiting the nurseries to work with their staff. A few authorities have been experimenting with the use of joint nursery school/day nurseries (" combined centres ") and it has sometimes been possible for day nurseries/day centres and nursery school/classes to be built sufficiently close to each other to encourage the development of co-operative working. Grouping facilities together should not, however, lead to their becoming so large or formal as to deter those who might use them.

19. Because of the limited number of places available in day nurseries priority for places is given to those with special need, including children of working lone parents, children with a mental or physical handicap, or whose home environment is so impoverished or so strained that they need day care and those whose parents are, through illness or handicap, unable to look after them during the day. The priorities observed in allocating day nursery places have led to special problems in looking after the children, and also to much work having to be centred on the parents whose difficulties with child rearing may be compounded by low income, inadequate housing and lack of community support. The NNEB certificate, while giving trainees an excellent basic knowledge of normal child development does not fully prepare them for work with parents and with children who have multiple problems. Authorities are therefore asked to ensure that so far as is possible senior staff appointed to day nurseries either hold, or are encouraged to obtain the CSS or CQSW qualifications.

20. Regular health surveillance is of importance for children in all forms of day care both as individuals and as members of an age-group which presents particular health hazards. Health visitors need to co-ordinate the care given to a child at home and in day care. The Departments therefore wish to emphasise the need for maintaining close links between health staff and all those (including child-minders) providing care for the children and for the latter to be particularly alert to any need to refer children in their care for medical investigation or treatment.

Playgroups

21. Playgroups provide the opportunity for parents and their children to come together in a flexible and informal setting so that the parents can work together with their own and other children and the children themselves are able to mix and play with each other. They therefore offer the opportunity for valuable social experience for parents and children. Social Services Departments with whom playgroups are required to be registered, are asked, if they have not already done so, to consider designating a member of their staff to examine with local voluntary groups how support and guidance for playgroups should best be provided. Social Services Departments are in any case asked to provide the Area Nurse (Child Health) at Area Health Authorities with the names and addresses of playgroups.

22. Playgroups will vary in terms of the contributions that they can make to the educational process because of differences between both the personalities involved and the premises and equipment available. Some of the parents concerned with the organisation and running of the playgroups may have been trained as social workers or teachers, some may have benefited from courses for playgroup leaders; but others may have received little or no guidance on the problems of organising the play of children to provide learning opportunities. Playgroups generally should have the benefit of contact with schools and teachers and of the knowledge and experience of the local education authority; the message of paragraph 17 of DES Circular 2/73 encouraging support for playgroups by local education authorities is particularly relevant, especially at a time when the rate of expansion of nursery education is inevitably slower than envisaged earlier.

23. While playgroups sometimes operate in the houses of play leaders, in health clinics and in village or church halls, an increasing number of authorities are making schools or other premises available to them, are providing equipment and materials, and are helping in other ways to set up new playgroups. A major factor where school premises are to be used is that heads and staff are often prepared not only to provide accommodation but to co-operate fully with these groups. A number of points, including the particular classroom to be used by playgroups and the location and suitability of lavatories, washing facilities and secure outside play space, need careful consideration.

Child-minders

24. The flexibility of child-minding has advantages for the working parent in that it may more readily be arranged to suit hours of work, and the minding arrangement can continue once a child has started school, with the minder providing care during out of school hours and school holidays. It is often nearer home than other provision, and can be related to the particular needs of children for whom other forms of day care may be unsuitable. From the child's point of view a good minder can provide him with informal care in familiar surroundings that is the nearest substitute to his own home, and also give him the opportunity to form the close, continuing relationships which much research has shown to be important for his development; for many children under 3 and those with special problems this is much more in tune with their limited capacity for social contacts than the communal experience of a day nursery.

25. The Nurseries and Child-Minders Regulation Act 1948 empowers Social Services Departments to register child-minders and to make conditions to ensure the adequate care of the child.

Authorities are therefore invited to review their support and advice services, including in-service training, for child-minders. It is also emphasised that where such support can be provided for registered minders it can serve to underline the advantages of registration, and so assist authorities in introducing minimum requirements for registration, designed to effect an overall improvement in the standard and image of child-minding in an area. Close liaison with the relevant health authorities is also recommended so as to ensure that the health needs of these children are not overlooked. Social Services Departments should also provide the Area Nurse (Child Health) at the Area Health Authorities with the names and addresses of minders and the children in their care so that health surveillance can be maintained. Similarly, because children who are merely minded are more likely than other children to be denied the social and intellectual stimulation that is important to their development, the Departments attach great importance to fostering links between child-minders and nursery schools, classes and teachers, with child health clinics and with voluntary groups working in this field—pre-school playgroups and toy libraries for example. Such links can help to break down the isolation experienced by many minders as well as broaden the experience of the children in their care.

26. Day fostering/sponsored child-minding schemes have been started by a number of authorities. Under these schemes local authorities recruit and pay allowances to selected people to look after young children under five, most of whom are within the priority day care groups, for the day or part of a day. The Departments invite local authorities to consider the introduction of schemes of this sort more widely as a complement to, but not necessarily as a cheaper substitute for, day nursery facilities. In the towns day foster parents can provide a service more suited to the needs of younger children and those in need of a more homely environment than can be provided at day nurseries. In the country, besides fulfilling this role, they can provide day care for families where demand is insufficient to justify building and staffing a day nursery. Day fostering schemes develop a sense of loyalty and pride in their work amongst the minders engaged in them, and can raise the standard and status of child-minding generally.

Conclusion

27. This circular letter indicates approaches to provision for the under-fives which have been adopted by some local authorities. The Departments hope that these approaches and the examples of local practice in the Annex will be of assistance to authorities generally in considering what further action they can take, within the limit of available resources, to achieve closer liaison between the various organisations concerned with the under-fives, including volunteers and voluntary organisations active in this field. The Departments would be glad if local authorities would send them for wider dissemination further examples of what has been achieved through local co-ordination. They would also welcome information on the experience of those local authorities who have set up joint advisory committees on the under-fives.

Yours faithfully

A C Clarke

Department of Health and
Social Security

Children's Division B
Alexander Fleming House
Elephant and Castle
London SE1 6BY

Tel. 01-407 5522 Ext. 6397

E B Granshaw

Department of Education
and Science

Schools Branch 1
Elizabeth House
York Road
London SE1 7PH

Tel. 01-928 9222 Ext. 3391

EXAMPLES OF CO-ORDINATION IN LOCAL PRACTICE

Links between schools, day nurseries, day centres and health services

1. In some areas joint planning and availability of suitable sites have enabled day nurseries/day centres, and nursery schools/classes to be built sufficiently close to each other for co-operative working to develop. In one area a trust has built a centre, which includes a day nursery, a mother and toddler club, a health clinic for mothers and pre-school children and a nursery school. The centre is managed by the Social Services Department in conjunction with the Education and Health Authorities which have particular responsibility for the school and health clinic respectively. Even where there is physical separation provision can still be jointly planned as in one area where a nursery unit attached to an infant school has been combined with a nursery class in a day centre half a mile away to provide 85 full-time equivalent places. Ten places are reserved for children from the day centre who are selected by its supervisor, but the educational element is the responsibility of the headteacher of the infant school.

2. More commonly, existing schools and day nurseries and centres have developed their activities beyond their traditional roles. For instance one inner city community school with a nursery unit has developed a considerable range of activities arising out of its formal nursery provision. Two nursery teachers, as well as teaching the children in the nursery unit, undertake home visiting with a particular emphasis on language development, advise a pre-school playgroup, support a child-minders' group and provide a Saturday morning nursery session. At the same school a health clinic for mothers and pre-school children is provided. At another school where children are drawn from a variety of ethnic groups classes on a wide range of subjects including language are provided for mothers while their children attend the school. In a number of areas, so as to extend the hours for which children are cared for, arrangements have been made in nursery classes for children to remain, under supervision, after school hours either within the class itself or, in the case of an urban authority, in one of the area's day centres.

3. Some day centres have incorporated special features including the provision of transport for children and mothers and/or child-minders, language classes and literacy tuition, courses to improve the quality of child care, libraries and toy lending services and health care and advice. One centre where health care and advice is available also provides a locus for meetings of day care advisers from voluntary and statutory agencies working locally.

4. A rather different example of co-ordination is that of a hospital day nursery run jointly by the Social Services Department and the Health Authority where the former is allocated places for which it bears proportionate costs.

5. In recognition of the educational needs of children who attend day nurseries, at least one authority plans to employ peripatetic teachers to visit these nurseries and work with their staff for a proportion of their time. In other authorities nurseries have close links with primary schools and visits to the schools are arranged to improve continuity between pre-school and school experiences. Not all links with schools are, however, at primary level; some secondary schools encourage a few older pupils to participate in the care of under fives at day nurseries during school hours. Such experience, when carefully planned with the secondary school pupils and the nursery staff, is of value not only to the nursery children but also to the secondary school pupils as potential parents.

Support for child-minders by local authority departments, health services, voluntary bodies and schools

6. In some areas arrangements exist under which children in the care of child-minders attend nursery schools and classes. Generally, where health visitors know that children from families whom they are visiting are being cared for by child-minders, wherever possible they also visit the children at the minder's home and give general advice to the minder on health matters relating to the children in her care. Many authorities have started toy libraries for child-minder groups. One Headmistress provides an additional service for child-minders: working together with the Social Services Department of her authority, she provides a weekly informal session for child-minders in her infant school. This is attended by an experienced nursery teacher and brings in nursery nursing students who visit the minders in their homes to introduce play ideas. One authority is planning a day nursery, with a group of child-minders attached, who will be supervised by the nursery. The nursery will provide a back-up service for holidays and periods of illness and emphasis is also to be placed on provision for families, particularly where mothers need support in the care of their children. In a number of areas the organisers of playgroups, in conjunction with the Social Services Department, are encouraging minders to come to playgroups with their children. In one authority a full-time officer supports child-minders and playgroups and is responsible for liaison with the Area Health Authority as well as with the Local Education Authority's advisory teachers for playgroups; he is also involved with playgroup teacher training.

Provision by Local Authorities, Health Services and Voluntary Bodies of Support for Families

7. Two projects aimed at developing home links are specifically designed to help parents develop the learning skills of their children. Under these projects visits are made to the homes of pre-school children selected from GP or health centre lists. Elsewhere teachers are employed on play buses which visit blocks of flats and introduce parents and children to pre-school facilities which might otherwise be denied them.

8. In other authorities home-link schemes have been established to foster links between home and school. In one authority an adult institute and a nursery school (in co-operation with the Social Services Department) have developed a scheme for visiting mothers of children who are likely to go to the nursery school. The home visitors provide help with play ideas. In another, a teacher has been appointed by an infant school with the specific job of visiting and working with pre-school children in its catchment area in their homes. This project concentrates on language development as the core of its activities and careful records of visits are maintained. When social problems arise a social worker is contacted.

9. Links with families are not, however, always dependent on visits to the home and in many areas parents are encouraged to attend, and become involved with nursery schools, classes and centres.

10. Voluntary organisations also have much to contribute to the development of home links. One organisation has the specific aim of helping families with young children to help themselves. Local groups of parents and their children meet each week and examine the ways in which they are bringing up their children and together learn from the results. This organisation is controlled by a committee, comprising representatives from the groups and from professional agencies, which provides support and guidance to the neighbourhood groups by hiring meeting places, paying running costs of crèches and by providing short weekend breaks for mothers and their children. Health, education and social services have been involved as has the local university and church. The organisation has made weekly broadcasts on local radio in which issues relating to early childhood development have been discussed.

11. A scheme in another area provides support for mothers experiencing difficulty with bringing up their children by arranging for volunteers to visit mothers referred by health visitors and

Social Services Departments. The volunteers, themselves parents, are supported by a team including representatives from the Social Services Department, Local Education Authority, Health Authority and the voluntary workers bureau and on their visits use their experience and skills to help the mothers gain self confidence and understanding of the needs of young children. Some of the mothers who have been helped through the scheme have themselves subsequently become visitors. In another area, at a family clinic, a team consisting of a psychologist, a medical officer, a health visitor, and a voluntary play leader offers help to parents and young children with problems, and works closely with the primary care team. The foregoing examples are likely to aid inter alia, in the prevention and treatment of early psychological problems in young children. Child Guidance services are also becoming increasingly involved with children under five. The multi-disciplinary team of psychiatrist, social worker and psychologist are extending their work into the community, and as well as direct assessment and treatment of families are providing a consultative service to health visitors, clinical medical officers and others concerned with the young child.

12. Elsewhere, a team of voluntary workers has been recruited and attached to the Social Services Department to give help and support to families that are restricted in their day to day living because of commitment to dependent relatives. This scheme encompasses families with members who are elderly or infirm, or mentally or physically handicapped as well as those where, because of divorce, separation or death, a single parent has a restricted social life through having to care for a large family.

Support for Playgroups by Local Authority Departments, Voluntary Agencies and Health Services

13. Many local authorities employ their own playgroup advisers. Elsewhere advisers from voluntary organisations also act as peripatetic playleaders and a voluntary organisation provides a forum within which playgroup organisers discuss experiences and problems. Peripatetic teachers also contribute to the educational element in playgroups in at least one area. In one rural authority all infant and nursery heads spend one session each week visiting playgroups in their area where they work alongside the supervisors giving advice and support. In another more compact area the head of an infant school or infant department is released to visit and advise playgroups. Arrangements for health visitors to be linked to playgroups are made by the majority of Health Authorities.

14. Authorities provide financial assistance for the playgroup movement in a number of forms *e.g.*:

— block grants to reduce either the general level of fees charged by individual playgroups, or in some instances, to subsidise places for individual children.

— rent-free accommodation.

— access to the authorities' bulk buying facilities.

Voluntary groups in some areas also provide transport to take children to playgroups.

15. Some Local Education Authorities, who are allowing playgroups to use spare school accommodation, have found it necessary—in conjunction with Social Services Departments—to lay down general guidelines for such arrangements. One authority stipulates that:

(a) the playgroup's committee shall include the head of the school and a representative of the managers if they wish;

(b) the playgroup's leader shall be suitably trained;

(c) the playgroups shall be open to inspection by the authority's officers; and

(d) charges shall be approved by, and accounts submitted for inspection to, the authority.

In a number of authorities teenagers assist in playgroups as part of secondary school or college of education courses. In one authority a joint working party, comprising local authority and voluntary agency representatives has drawn up guidelines for the use of schools and playgroups on the involvement of secondary school students in playgroups.

16. Schemes have been developed by a voluntary agency in several areas to develop contacts with travellers and their children through the provision of playgroups. These have assisted in introducing the families to other facilities provided by local and health authorities.

Support for Mother and Baby Clubs by Local Authority Departments, Health Services and Schools

17. Mother and Toddler Clubs and similar groups complement playgroup and nursery school provision. Clubs have been set up in child health clinics and infant schools, by a number of authorities.

Many clubs are organised by voluntary agencies and the mothers themselves. These clubs provide the opportunity to break down the social isolation experienced by many parents with very young children.

Support for the Handicapped provided by Local Authority Departments, Health Services, Voluntary Bodies and Schools

18. At comprehensive assessment centres, organised by Health Authorities in many areas, multi-disciplinary teams assess the needs of, and co-ordinate services for, handicapped children. An essential feature of the services provided by the centres is to bring together all those concerned from the health service, local authority and voluntary agencies so as to facilitate the multi-disciplinary assessment of a handicapped child's needs and enable regular reassessments to be made. In this way, in the light of the child's growth and development and his response to treatment, training and education and to his environment, optimum help and support can be arranged for the child and his family.

19. In support of Local Education Authorities, in their responsibility for the assessment of handicapped children over the age of 2 for education, health and social services staff are co-operating closely with education authorities' staff in the running of nursery schools and classes attached to special and ordinary schools. Opportunity groups run by voluntary groups and local authorities are also in many areas, providing new experiences for handicapped children which help to widen their horizons and also to reduce stress in their families. Suitable play material is provided in these groups, and in some instances toy libraries also provide the opportunity for similar toys to be available in the children's homes. Referrals to the playgroups are made by health visitors and social workers.

20. Handicapped children should have much to gain from sharing the school resources available to non-handicapped children; some local authorities help parents to meet transport costs. In many areas playgroups have been set up specifically to meet the needs of handicapped pre-school children. The groups are run by volunteers—who often include the parents of children attending—and are strongly supported by local authorities, in some cases with advice from their advisory teachers. The groups not only help the children but also provide support for their families.

21. In many authorities peripatetic teachers of the deaf and teachers and advisers of the visually handicapped are working with pre-school children in their homes, and in clinics, hospitals, nurseries and other day care facilities, as well as in schools and nursery classes. A voluntary agency is providing a number of advisers whose work complements that of Local Education Authorities' advisers of the visually handicapped. Some local authorities have appointed advisory teachers for pre-school handicapped children. These teachers liaise with social workers, health authorities and voluntary groups so that there is optimum development of the learning skills of handicapped children and provision of advice and training for parents.

22. In one rural authority, partially hearing children who are having treatment, or who are under observation, are brought to see the ENT consultant in his room, which is in the same building as a nursery school, at appropriate intervals accompanied by their parent and teacher. This applies whether the child is in a special or ordinary school. The teacher and consultant together discuss the progress and treatment of the child with the parent listening and contributing. In another area pre-school speech and language units have been set up by the speech therapy service assisted by volunteer help largely provided by the parents of the children concerned. An educational psychologist and medical officer are also involved.

23. In another area a voluntary organisation and the Social Services Department jointly provide support for families with deaf children and arrange for parents with newly diagnosed deaf children to be visited by those who have had experience of bringing up a deaf child.

Co-ordination of Training Provision for Playgroup-Personnel and Child-Minders

24. Training courses for playgroup supervisors and parents who take part in playgroups are now well established in many areas and are provided by a range of institutions including universities. In one rural authority training courses are provided on an inter-disciplinary basis and involve teachers, social workers and health visitors and the courses are open to both parents and pre-school playgroup supervisors. In other authorities courses are open to child-minders. Many authorities' adult education institutes provide training for playgroup personnel and provide playgroup facilities for the children of those attending playgroup courses. A number of adult and further education institutes engage full-time staff who assist playgroups; local teaching staff also contribute. In one area a joint working party comprising education, social services and a voluntary organisation have produced a syllabus for a basic ten-week course which is accepted and provided throughout the area for child-minders, foster parents and parents involved in playgroups.

25. Training is provided for registered child-minders in an increasing number of areas, sometimes formally through the adult education and further education system, and sometimes less formally as when minders meet together in groups to view films and/or hold discussions both between themselves and with the professional workers. In such instances their children are cared for by the staff of the schools or day nurseries alongside the nursery school or day nursery children. Minders' husbands join in some groups in the evenings and at weekends and their contribution to the care of the minded children is explored. Some authorities are also arranging for the parents of the minded children to join minders' training sessions but without skilful handling this may lead to difficulties.

26. Many of the groups of child minders organised by Social Services Departments and voluntary organisations to view together the recent BBC television series " Other People's Children ", have become more permanent and are continuing to meet. They provide a useful means of alleviating the isolation frequently experienced by both minders and the children in their care and also enable minders to increase their knowledge and understanding of child care. The Open University, the Health Education Council and the Pre-School Playgroups Association have set up courses for parents of pre-school children.

UNITED KINGDOM GENERAL GOVERNMENT EXPENDITURE FOR THE MAIN SOCIAL PROGRAMMES SHOWING APPROXIMATE EXPENDITURE DIRECTLY ATTRIBUTABLE TO 0–15 YEAR OLDS AND 0–4 YEAR OLDS—1976

£ million

	Total current and capital	Total current only (excluding current grants abroad)	Amounts directly attributable to 0–15 year olds	Amounts attributed to 0–4 year olds
Main social programmes:				
Education...	7,794	7,050	4,825(a)	175
Health	6,182	5,752	924(b)	440
Personal Social Services	1,128	1,034	330(c)	85
Social Security	11,233	11,153	615(d)	150
Libraries, Museums, Arts	329	292	31(e)	—
Total	26,666	25,281	6,725	850

NOTES

General:

As specified in the title, the figures in the last columns are those estimated as being *directly* attributable to children up to the minimum school-leaving age. It should be noted that there are some large expenditure programmes which cannot be so attributed. For example, some £300 million of the Housing and Environmental Services programme was devoted to parks, pleasure grounds and recreational facilities much used by children within the age group. Other programmes similarly affected are Transport and Communication, other parts of Housing and Environmental Services, Police, Parliament and Law Courts, and Records, Registrations and Surveys. The estimate for Social Security does not include the loss of Central Government revenue through Child Tax Allowances, of the order of £1,000 million in 1976.

Details:

(a) Education consists of expenditure on nursery, primary, secondary and special schools; child guidance; youth service and physical training; transport of pupils; school meals, milk and welfare foods; administration; and an estimate of the cost of school crossing patrols.

(b) Health consists of hospital and community health services; family practitioner services; and administration.

(c) PSS consists of residential accommodation; day nurseries; boarding out; social work; home helps; intermediate treatment; other local authority spending; and administration.

(d) Social Security consists of family allowances; attendance allowance; guardian allowance; child's special allowance; and administration.

(e) Estimated cost of children's books added to stock during year at public libraries.

Produced in England for Her Majesty's Stationery Office
by City Litho Printers Ltd, Stroud